MW00648323

Retiring Upstream

Finding Happiness and Security in the Transition of a Lifetime

Alan Kondo, CFP™, CLU, CCA
Akemi Kondo Dalvi, CPA

This publication is designed to provide accurate and authoritative information in regard to the subject matter covered. While legal, tax, accounting, charitable and financial planning information covered in this book has been checked for accuracy, some material may be affected by changes in the laws or in the interpretation of such laws since the book was published. For this reason, the accuracy and completeness of such information and the opinions based thereon are not guaranteed. In addition, state or local tax laws or procedural rules may have a material impact on the general recommendations made by the authors, and the strategies outlined in this book may not be suitable for every individual. If legal, accounting, financial planning or other expert advice is required, the services of a competent professional should be sought.

CFP™ and Certified Financial Planner™ are certification marks owned by the Certified Financial Planner Board of Standards, Inc.

CLU and Chartered Life Underwriter are certification marks owned by the American College.

CCA and Certified Collaborative Advisor are certification marks owned by WealthCounsel®.

CPA and Certified Public Accountant are certifications administered by the National Association of State Boards of Accountancy (NASBA)

ISBN: 978-0-615-86688-8

DEDICATION

ALAN:

To my wife Ruth Wakabayashi
for her constant friendship, wisdom and encouragement.
My life is richer and has greater meaning because of you.

To my daughters Kimiko, Akemi and Masayo
for blessing others with your
selflessness, courage and kindness.

To my parents, Harry and Yuki Kondo
who gave me the values to guide my life,
the support to carry them out,
and the confidence to believe in myself.

AKEMI:

To my father, who is a great teacher and mentor,
and to my mother, Susan,
who loves unconditionally,
in the way only a mother can.

To my husband, Ashay,
for your steadfast support, and true friendship.
To my son, Aiden, for giving me drive and purpose in life.

TABLE OF CONTENTS

v

ACKNOWLEDGEMENTS

We would like to thank our staff for their support and enthusiasm as we wrote this book. Thank you Joanie, Jeannette, Susan, Alice, Suki and Christina. Thank you to our marketing consultant Tasha Kaji for the book title and cover design – your creativity has no bounds.

The advice in this book is a summary of what attorneys, CPAs and other Certified Financial Planners™ have shared with us. The guidance we give our clients is only possible because of your generosity.

Thank you to the Rafu Shimpo newspaper and editor Gwen Muranaka for your commitment as a voice and advocate for the Japanese American community.

We were honored to have community leaders like Leslie Ito, Ken Kasamatsu, Shawn Miyake and Alan Nishio make time in their hectic schedules to review this book. Your valuable feedback has helped to make it more relevant and your ongoing advice has helped to keep KWA on the right track.

Thank you to Leslie Strebel, EMyth coach, for guiding our growth over the last eleven years, and helping us to navigate the next chapter for Kondo Wealth Advisors.

Investment management firm Loring Ward has been one of the most important arrows in our quiver for providing broad, global diversification and balance of asset classes to our clients. Thank you for going above and beyond your role to become a trusted resource in building our practice.

Thank you to Schwab Advisor Services and Schwab Institutional for helping us make a successful transition to become an independent Registered Investment Advisor. Our goal to provide excellent service to our clients would not be possible without Schwab's support and customer service.

We would like to thank our clients who have opened their hearts to us, sharing their pearls of wisdom and life experiences to help others make better decisions. Your real-life stories helped the book come alive. Thank you especially to our clients Will and Laura Edwards, Ken and JoAnn Hamamura, John and Betty Hatakeyama, Mark Mayeda and Debbie Ching who gave us candid feedback on the content and titling of our book.

Achieving retirement goals sometimes feels like swimming against the current. The struggle to forge ahead is similar to the koi's legendary ability to climb waterfalls and overcome obstacles. We titled the book *Retiring Upstream* because events like the tech bubble, the housing bubble and the Great Recession have been considerable obstacles in many people's journey towards retirement. We hope this book will help readers transition from their working life to retirement smoothly and successfully.

Japanese Americans, in particular, have had to rebuild their financial lives several times: after the first generation arrived in the United States, after the Great Depression, and after being incarcerated in U.S. concentration camps during World War II. This book is written with special attention to Japanese American history, community and culture, but the financial advice and strategies can help everyone gain a more secure and fulfilling retirement.

Long before I made financial planning my profession, I was badly in need of financial advice myself. I made an appointment with a financial advisor, went to his plush office and sat across his polished, walnut desk. However when I started to explain my goals and challenges, expectations and fears, he seemed disinterested. Instead of addressing what I wanted, he launched into a monologue filled with technical jargon about how he managed investments.

Then he tried to sell me an annuity. Unsure about how this product would help me to achieve my goals, I declined. He gave me a somber look. "I'm sorry," he said, "I don't think I can help you."

In his opinion, I wasn't a very good fit for his practice and didn't meet the characteristics that defined a good client. The experience was very discouraging.

I realized then that financial planning is a very personal business. It's not only about money. It's about understanding people's hopes and dreams, caring enough to help them do the best for them and their families, and then harnessing the right financial strategies and products to make their dreams come true.

When I started Kondo Wealth Advisors, it was my intention to serve everyone, but pay special attention to the Japanese American community, which I felt was underserved. I understood the history and culture of our community well, and this enabled me to make better recommendations than an advisor who didn't understand these subtleties. It was like working with my family, and indeed many of my clients have become good friends.

This book is a continuation of my earlier one, *Path To Antei: A Japanese American Guide to Financial Success* which came out in 2003. Some sections from the old book that were still relevant have been included in this publication, but everything has been updated to account for the quickly-changing tax laws and the impact of the Great Recession.

What's new is the focus on retirement planning. Most of our clients are about to retire or are already retired, so it is an area that we know well. Retirement is one of the greatest challenges facing the Baby Boomer generation, a group of 60 million people reaching retirement at the rate of one every ten seconds for the next 15 years. For Japanese Americans, retirement poses special challenges because of our tradition of caring for elders, the high value we place on educating and nurturing future generations, and the importance we place on preserving our community.

At a time when the financial viability of government safety nets like Social Security and Medicaid (Medi-Cal in California) are questionable and defined benefit pension plans are as rare as honest politicians, no one can afford to make a mistake in their retirement planning.

Unlike learning how to ride a bicycle, we don't have the luxury of falling down several times and scraping our knees. The consequences of making a mistake are too dire. With retirement we have to get it right the first time. To do this we have to plan well and learn from the experience of other people.

This is especially true for Japanese Americans who for generations have been impeded from building financial security. Historically, Japanese Americans have had to start over several times. The first time was in the early 1900s when the Issei (first generation Japanese Americans) landed in the U.S. with little more than the shirts on their backs. They were welcomed with the 1913 Alien Land Law that barred Japanese Americans from owning land. It was an attempt to prevent Japanese Americans from gaining a foothold in farming, one of the few industries where they could be fairly compensated for their hard work.

Nevertheless, they persevered, supported each other during those hard times and managed to survive. Just when they were regaining their footing financially the rug was pulled out from under them by the Great Depression. Many families lost almost everything and had to start over.

These bleak times brought Japanese Americans closer together. They established Japanese Associations to unify the community and coordinate political and social activities. Instead of competing against each other, Japanese businesses often worked together so they could all do well.

Just when they were beginning to enjoy some prosperity and stability, Japanese American men, women and children were hauled off to U.S. concentration camps in the racist hysteria and economic plunder of World War II. Their land, businesses, equipment and belongings were sold for pennies on the dollar, and the farms that they had built from scratch to profitable ventures were snatched up by agribusiness. Many Nisei (second generation Japanese Americans) never finished their high school or college educations. After the war ended and they were released from the camps, Japanese Americans had to start over once more.

Dr. Mary Oda was a family practice physician in the San Fernando Valley for 47 years. During her career she estimates she delivered over 3,000 babies.

"When the war started we had all the crops planted. Within about six months we would have made a fortune, but we had to leave everything, including a tractor and a lot of equipment, to go to camp."

"During the time we were in camp, somebody farmed our land, but didn't pay a cent in rent. During the war, my father, brother and sister died. My sister died first. She developed asthma in camp. My father died next. He developed cancer of the throat. Then my brother died. Within seven months, all three had died."

"When we came back after the war, there was nothing left. They had stolen everything. The cars that we left, somebody drove them off. My brother had a stamp and coin collection. Somebody had broken in and it was all gone."

As a result of these setbacks, we have a few clients who are Japanese American multi-millionaires, but most of them are regular folks. They were employees at companies, worked as teachers and pharmacists, and started small businesses. They worked hard all their lives. Now that they are getting close to retirement, or have already retired, they want to make sure all their hard work is not squandered by a careless mistake or bad advice.

We feel that we have a responsibility to our clients and to our community. If we can help our clients steward their money well, it will strengthen the community. If we can enable our clients to pass assets successfully to their children, grandchildren and their favorite community organizations, it will advance the community's future.

I am proud to be joined in my practice and in this book by my daughter, Akemi Kondo Dalvi, CPA. She left PricewaterhouseCoopers six years ago to join me, and I am endlessly grateful. To find a financial planning partner that is competent, ethical and innovative is hard enough – to find one who also cares deeply about her clients and her community is a blessing. There are many Certified Financial Planners™ who are not so lucky and have no successor or succession plan. I hope that our clients will find peace of mind knowing that I have taken the steps to watch over their long-term well-being and carry the momentum of their good planning forward to assist their children and grandchildren.

When I have an initial meeting with our clients I ask them about their hopes and dreams. My greatest satisfaction comes from seeing them successfully enjoy the fruits of their labor many years later. When they are able to travel, spend time with their grandchildren, dig in the garden or support the community, I feel fortunate to be in a profession that can make a positive difference for so many people.

My decision to make a career transition to financial planning and investment management was a professional choice, but was of a personal nature as well. I've been told that it is a true blessing to love what you do, and my father always felt great about his work, even at the end of a long day.

I can relate it to the look he had on his face after a full day of fishing. He may have left the house at 5am and returned home at 8pm, sun-kissed and smelling like fish, but he came home feeling accomplished...and happy. I hoped that by joining him, I might be able to achieve the same trifecta of happiness: family, purpose, spirituality.

Prior to working at Kondo Wealth Advisors, I was a CPA with PricewaterhouseCoopers, LLP. I enjoyed the fast pace environment, the valuable training and the corporate experience. I am very grateful for the time I spent with PwC. When my father offered me the opportunity to join him and learn from his mentorship, it was an offer I couldn't refuse, so I made the leap. The transition was smooth. I was able to leverage the financial and tax training of my CPA credentialing into well-rounded, tax-conscious financial advice.

When my father asked me to write this book with him, I was initially nervous and reluctant. However, he explained that sharing knowledge was a responsibility to the community and that we were simply a stepping stone for others on their journey to a happy retirement. I was much more comfortable being a stepping stone and agreed to compile the lessons taught to me in what I hope will be of value to those looking for financial soundness.

The importance of the work we do struck home in 2010, when my husband and I welcomed our wonderful baby boy, Aiden, into our family. It was the most humbling feeling in the world. I finally realized I knew NOTHING about life (my mom waited a long time to hear that).

Everything changed: my drive to provide, my sleep, my outlook on life. Aiden was born with a congenital defect and the first year of his life was challenging, health-wise. However, his challenges connected my family and me to a deeper sense of spirituality as an American melting-pot family which consisted of Christians, Buddhists and Hindus. When we prayed together for a common good, it was a beautiful thing. I mention Aiden not only because his birth is the most significant occurrence in my life, but also because he helped me to understand the drive that many of our clients have to provide, not just financially over their own life expectancies, but for their kin, spiritually, personally and professionally.

In my profession, and in this book, I hope to impart people with the knowledge they need to prepare for their retirement successfully through proper planning, investing, and spending.

Many Sansei (third-generation Japanese Americans) and Yonsei (fourth-generation Japanese Americans) have grown up vastly different from their parents and grandparents generations. A good number were born and raised in a house in the suburbs and their families were often financially stable enough to allow them to go to college and perhaps even pursue a Master's Degree rather than going to work right out of high school to help support the family. After college, many took jobs that earned good salaries and accumulated wealth through hard work and maybe even some inheritances. However, what has been eye-opening is that affluence alone does not lead to financial soundness and long-term well-being. Unfortunately, we've seen how a few bad decisions can lead a hard-working couple to work longer than they had hoped or even worse, run out of money in retirement.

We found that much can be learned from our clients. In particular, a hard-working South Bay husband and wife come to mind. They visited our office for some advice on investing their retirement funds. He was a gardener and she worked as a secretary for a large corporation. They had a small home, lived modestly and drove used cars. They were your typical non-assuming JA couple. They asked us if we could help them manage their portfolio and handed over a few bank statements holding their savings accounts. We were floored to see they had close to a million dollars in savings. The wife explained that they had worked hard and saved diligently. They lived off of the husbands' income and socked her income into savings for retirement. She had earned company stock for her years of service and it had split a couple times and multiplied in value. They were the living example of what hard work and disciplined savings could provide. We admired them for making a plan and sticking to it!

What gives us comfort in our profession is that some financial direction can be achieved by setting reasonable goals, taking measured steps to achieve those goals, displaying a little discipline to defer short-term luxuries for long-term stability, and providing a little flexibility to adjust for the curve balls that life (or the financial market) throws our way.

We hope that through our book, we can help families to continue to navigate the financial jungle and avoid some unnecessary mishaps. With economic changes and tax law updates, it was necessary to re-examine strategies that will work best for our clients.

I love serving our clients because they are a part of our community and greater family. In many ways, they take care of me as much as I take care of them. I've found that I advise our clients on how to manage their investments, and in exchange, our clients guide me on how to live a full and meaningful life. They give me advice on navigating the ups and downs of parenthood, caring for aging family members, and most of all, they remind me to appreciate each day with my loved ones before they pass. I am forever grateful for their insight and wisdom.

CHAPTER 1

ARE YOU READY FOR RETIREMENT?

———————

B y most measures, retirement for this generation is more challenging and problematic than in previous generations. Many people who planned to retire in 2008 or 2009 were just about to reach the top of the mountain, when the mountain moved! A CNN study showed that since the Great Recession which started in 2008, two-thirds of potential retirees planned to postpone retirement. More than one-third were concerned that they might never be able to retire. They had good reason to worry.

Even without the recession, funding retirement has become a lot more difficult to achieve. One reason is that people are living a lot longer. Methuselah, the biblical character, lived to be 969 years old. While you may not live quite that long, recent statistics show that American life expectancy has increased 30 years during the 20th century alone. Research on fruit flies has extended their life expectancy to a human equivalent of 150 years. Can man be far behind? Living longer will have a significant impact on how you plan for retirement.

The good news is that not only are you likely to live much longer than you expected, you are probably going to be alert and healthy much longer than your parents' generation. We can hope that cancer and Alzheimer's disease will join the ranks of measles and tetanus, and no longer be the life alter-ing threat they represent today. The sacrifice that you made in previous decades through exercising and dieting will pay off in improved quality of life later on.

Gerontology studies have indicated that for a couple both age 65, there is a 50% chance that one of them will live beyond age 92 and a 25% chance that one of them will live beyond age 97. In other words, if you're both 65, plan on spending the next 30 years together!

Funding 30 years of retirement is a daunting prospect. The Nisei generation (second-generation Japanese Americans) had a much lower hurdle. Not only did they tend to work longer than retirees today, but they also didn't live as long. Consequently, they didn't have to fund as many years of re-tirement as we do today.

We may not be able to rely on entitlement programs like Social Security to bail us out if we run out of money dur-ing retirement. Back in 1935, when Roosevelt started Social Security, he declared that the government would help fund a comfortable retirement for everyone over age 65. He was secure in the knowledge that average life expectancy in 1935 was only 62, and most people in that generation were never going to enjoy the promise of Social Security.

Things have changed. In 1935, there were 40 people paying into Social Security for every 1 person who was taking money out. In 2020, there will be fewer than 2 people putting money into Social Security for every person who is receiving benefits (Ken Dychtwald, Age Wave). It is no wonder that so many people question whether Social Security will still be around by the time they retire. Many financial planners are reluctant to take Social Security benefits into account when they create retirement plans. If it's still there, it will be a welcome bonus.

For most people, their lifestyle in retirement will depend on how well prepared they are financially. Unfortunately, most people are very unprepared. Based on recent information, if you took 100 Americans age 25 and followed them to age 65, only 10 people would have more than $4,000 per year of retirement income. The other 90 would be either dead or dead broke. If you multiply this by the Baby Boomer retirement population, (those born between 1946-1964) it's not difficult to picture desperation in massive proportions.

Today's retirees must keep their eyes on dual goals – accumulating sufficient money to retire and keeping the money growing so it doesn't run out. The investment strategy you implement could help you accomplish both of these goals.

If you do like your parents did, keeping your retirement money in the bank or in other low-yielding investments like Treasury Bills or bonds, inflation will eat away at your return and your net gain may be flat or even negative. You'll be certain to get your investment back but over the course of 30 years you will have probably lost about two-thirds of your purchasing power. That's the price of certainty.

Another conventional wisdom is to sell off all your equity investments at retirement and replace them with bonds. This strategy no longer works because it increases the risk of running out of money. Many investors who have limited retirement resources can't afford to sacrifice return in order to gain safety.

Fortunately, there are better options available to today's investors; strategies that can provide more stable returns while reducing risk at the same time.

GET YOUR RETIREMENT BACK ON TRACK

The journey to retirement is like sailing around the world. Few long voyages end without encountering some rough seas. When you run into a bad storm, most everyone gets blown off-course. It's what you do afterwards that makes the difference. Experienced sailors figure out where they are and get back on course. It's the same with your retirement.

Many people look to the media for direction, but that's not usually very wise. The media has its own agenda. The media wants to keep you glued to the screen watching their commercials. To accomplish that, they stir up fear. They're very good at it, and it tends to make people panic. Panic often paralyzes people and prevents them from moving forward.

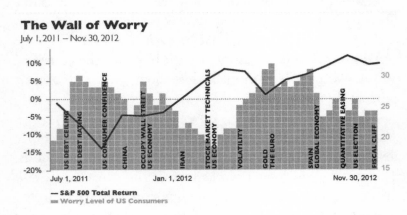

The Wall of Worry
July 1, 2011 – Nov. 30, 2012

— **S&P 500 Total Return**
— Worry Level of US Consumers

The media builds a Wall of Worry, but you can see from the chart above that the market continues to grow. When the media starts stirring up fear, talk to your Certified Financial Planner™ to find out what's really going on.

Your goals are probably still achievable. The problem is that most people have little idea where they currently stand, and how far they are from their goals. In order to get to the goal at Point B, you need to know where you are now at Point A. That's why it's important to create a Comprehensive Financial Plan.

The Comprehensive Financial Plan is constructed using a holistic approach taking into account all the elements of your financial life. This is because every piece of your financial life affects the other pieces – they're interconnected. In a well-constructed Comprehensive Financial Plan, the whole is stronger than any of the individual pieces.

A Comprehensive Financial Plan will answer the question of whether you need to delay retirement. You may find that you're not so far off track after all.

Even if you discover that you have to work a few more years, you'll have a lot of company. For Baby Boomers, the whole concept of retirement has become very different from their parents' retirement. A Rutgers study showed that 70% of retirees don't intend to play golf or watch television for the rest of their lives. Today's "retirement" often means doing some part-time work, consulting, volunteerism or even starting a business. Retired people today still want the satisfaction of a job well done, intellectual challenge and camaraderie – and they want to stay sharp!

The trend is even more pronounced for Baby Boomers. The Rutgers study found that 90% of Baby Boomers plan to stay active after retirement. The former chairman of Chrysler, Lee Iacocca, was known for his feisty and iconoclastic nature. He said about aging, "It takes until [age] 50 to know what the hell is going on in the world." He could well have been expressing the sentiments of Baby Boomers: "Now that we have all this wisdom and experience, why waste it?"

Financially, there are several benefits to working a little longer. According to the Social Security Administration, every year you delay retirement adds another 8% to your Social Security benefits. Compared to retiring early at age 62, if you wait until your normal retirement age of 66, your benefit will be 32% larger. If you delay to the maximum age of 70, your Social Security benefit will be 64% higher.

Working a few more years also gives you the opportunity to contribute more to your Qualified Retirement Plan. If you're an employee of a corporation, you probably have a 401(k). If you work for a non-profit organization, an educational institution or a hospital, you may have a 403(b) plan (also called TSAs). Many governmental organizations use 457 Deferred Compensation plans. They work similarly. If you're not in any of these categories you can still contribute to an Individual Retirement Account or IRA.

Continuing contributions to your 401(k), 403(b), 457 or IRA can make a big difference to your retirement nest egg. Let's say you're 62 years old and you keep working to age 67. If you continue to contribute 15% annual income into your retirement savings you can end up with 44% more retirement income. If you keep working to age 70, your retirement income increases by nearly 80%. This is because you are not only increasing your retirement savings, you are also shortening the number of years you need to fund retirement.

An added benefit is the opportunity to shift the cost of healthcare to your employer for a few more years. As you may be aware, the cost of healthcare insurance is substantial. This is what prevents many people from retiring early – they lose their group medical benefits when they retire but they're still too young for Medicare, which starts at age 65. Sock away what you would have spent in healthcare costs and put it into your retirement plan.

PUT YOUR SAVINGS ON AUTOPILOT

One of the secrets to getting back on track is to invest systematically. In other words, set up automatic monthly contributions into an investment. Following are some easy ways to save for the future.

Einstein called financial compounding the "8th Wonder of the World." Compounding is what happens when your money earns interest and then your money plus the interest earns more interest, growing larger and larger like a rolling financial snowball. Unfortunately, many people don't take advantage of this powerful phenomenon because they don't understand how systematic savings work.

You've heard the phrase, "Pay yourself first." Most people save what's left over after they've paid the bills. If you're like most people, there's rarely anything left over. Years can pass without anything going into savings. Can you afford to save $5.50

a day? It could be as simple as one less Venti Mocha with Whipped Cream per day. You can also save $5.50 per day by bringing lunch from home instead of buying it at work.

Your waistline and your portfolio will thank you. That $5.50 per day represents annual savings of $2,000 per year. Does the result seem a little paltry for all that sacrifice? Take a look at the long-term effects. I give the following example to the children and grandchildren of our clients.

Suppose Joanie, 21 years old, puts away $2,000 per year every year until she turns 30. Then she stops, having invested a total of $18,000. Without putting in another penny she just lets the $18,000 compound and earn 11% per year (the average return for the Standard and Poor's 500 since its inception) until she reaches age 65. It will have grown to $1,092,748! It's an easy way to become a millionaire. Keep in mind that this example does not include any brokerage fees or commissions. You cannot invest directly into the S&P 500, since it is an unmanaged index, but there are mutual funds and exchange-traded funds that replicate it.

By comparison, suppose Glenn waited until he turned age 31 to start saving. He then started putting away $2,000 per year and continued the annual contributions all the way to age 65. He would have contributed a total of $68,000. At age 65 he would have a total of $613,675 assuming the same rate of return. Note that this is much less than Joanie's example, even though Glenn put in $50,000 more.

Would you rather put in $18,000 to get $1,092,748, or $68,000 to get $613,675? It's a no-brainer. If you want to take maximum advantage of the leverage of compounding, start as soon as possible. Of course, the best scenario is to start at age 21 and put away $2,000 per year all the way to age 65. You could end up with a whopping $1,775,925!

It's possible to put this process on autopilot. What if your $5.50 per day were automatically deducted from your paycheck? And what if it only cost you $4 to save $5.50? This is how employer-sponsored retirement plans, like a 401(k), 403(b) or 457 plan, work. Many employees who are eligible to participate in these plans have not yet started. It's a big mistake not to participate.

The amount you elect to save is deducted from your paycheck on a pre-tax basis. Because this salary reduction also reduces your income tax, it only costs you about $4 to save $5.50 at the 28% tax bracket. It's as if Uncle Sam were helping you to save. In addition, the money will grow tax-deferred, meaning that you won't be taxed on interest, dividends or capital gains until you start taking out the money in retirement. Even better, some companies will partially match what you put in (for example fifty cents for each dollar of the employee's contributions, up to a ceiling, usually 6% of compensation) leveraging the value of your contributions even more.

In a 401(k), 403(b) or 457 plan, you are responsible for selecting the investment choices from a menu of options. In other words, you have to be your own investment manager. The basic rules of investing still apply. The key is diversification (not putting all your eggs in one basket). Many plans offer limited investment options but employees often make the situation worse by choosing only two or three mutual funds. Each fund is comprised of 100-200 different companies, however, often these funds overlap and invest in the same companies.

Another common mistake is to invest everything in lower-returning fixed-income options (bonds). Bonds have their place in a diversified portfolio but putting 100% into bonds will cause your retirement plan to lag behind annual inflation. You don't want to lose purchasing power each year.

Employers are supposed to provide investment education and advice to their employees so they can make the best decisions, but many times this guidance is perfunctory or non-existent. If this is the case in your company, ask your Certified Financial Planner™ to help you select from the investment options and construct the best asset allocation.

Don't invest too much of your 401(k) in your company stock. Roughly one-third of 401(k) assets are placed in company stock, according to Hewitt Associates. It's not unusual to find employees holding nearly all of their plan assets in company stock, and then doubling down by holding additional stock options outside of the 401(k).

An unexpected, dramatic decline in the value of your company's stock could force you back to work if you've retired. If you haven't retired yet, you could be faced with the double whammy of losing your job and your nest egg at the same time.

Enron workers learned this the hard way back in 2004, and it was a lesson for all of us. Many of the Enron employees had a substantial amount of Enron stock in their 401(k) accounts. When Enron started collapsing, they desperately wanted to sell their stock because it was falling in value daily.

The company froze the 401(k), preventing anyone from doing any trading. Ironically, during this same period, the executives of Enron were selling off their stock as quickly as they could.

We're not suggesting that your company is like Enron, but the truth of the matter is that over 25 to 30 years of retirement, you never know what can happen to your old company. Overweighting your 401(k) in company stock exposes you to increased risk.

How much company stock is appropriate? Around 10% or less of your overall 401(k) might be suitable, but you should consult with your CFP™ because everyone's circumstances and goals are different. Be aware that many companies match your contributions in company stock, so it may be tricky to keep it at 10%. Your company may also encourage employees to buy company stock by offering it at a special discount.

Companies often restrict the sale of company stock. You may not be able to sell it before a certain age, such as 50; you may be required to hold it for a certain time, such as five years; or you may be required to hold a certain percentage, such as two to four times salary if you are a senior executive. You should check your plan for specific details.

WHAT IF YOU DON'T HAVE A 401(K)?

If you don't qualify for an employer-sponsored plan, you can make automatic, monthly contributions to an IRA, preferably by systematic transfers from your bank account. The IRS places a cap on annual IRA contributions. Once you've maxed out your IRA, you can continue to make contributions to a non-IRA brokerage account.

Why do we emphasize monthly contributions? It's an investing strategy called Dollar Cost Averaging. Because you're putting the same amount of money away each month, it gives you a statistical advantage. If the market is down for the month, your money buys more shares because the shares are cheaper. If the market is up for the month, you are purchasing fewer shares because they are more expensive. Consequently, you are buying more when it's cheap, and less when it's expensive. This is one way to make the volatility of the market work for you. Over time, Dollar Cost Averaging can make a significant, positive difference in your bottom-line return.

Remember, Dollar Cost Averaging involves continuous investment regardless of fluctuating price levels. Doing regular, monthly contributions that you don't have to think about is one of the most effective, painless ways to save. In most cases, you won't even miss the money that has gone into your investment. When you happen to look at the balance in your retirement account, you may be pleasantly shocked at how much you've accumulated.

There's a story about a man who was lost in the desert and had a vision. A genie came to him and said, "Fill your pockets with as much sand as you can carry. At the end of your journey you will be filled with both pleasure and regret." The man did as he was told and stuffed his pockets, but not too much because the sand was heavy and he was already exhausted. He finally made his way out of the desert, and when he looked in his pockets he was amazed to find that the sand had turned to gold. He was filled with pleasure at his good fortune and filled with regret that he hadn't taken more sand. Don't be filled with regret. Create a savings plan for yourself, start as early as you can, and be disciplined about sticking to your plan.

CHAPTER 2

WHAT IS RETIREMENT PLANNING?

A common misconception is that you have to be a multimillionaire before it's worthwhile to hire a financial planner. While it's true that some financial planners only work with clients who have high net worth, there are many financial planners who purposely design their practices to serve the middle class. The fact is that everyone can make better decisions about their money by receiving professional guidance.

Retirement planning can give you the ability to balance and realize multiple goals in one of the most complex transitions of your life. It can help you gain financial independence so that you have more than enough income to cover all your expenses and do all the things that bring you pleasure and fulfillment. It can make sure that any emergencies, accidents or illnesses are anticipated and taken care of. It can create security for your children and grandchildren. Finally, it can enhance your ability to help others and benefit your community.

There are important areas that a Certified Financial Planner™ generally covers:
- cash flow planning
- tax planning
- investment planning
- financial independence planning

- insurance planning
- special situations

In many cases, a planner will help his or her clients balance competing goals, such as saving for retirement while putting children through college and helping out elderly parents at the same time. Because a CFP™ typically looks at the big picture, rather than individual bits and pieces, he or she is able to make sure the various parts are working in harmony and that the comprehensive plan does not achieve one goal at the expense of another.

Most Certified Financial Planners™ will offer an initial consultation without charge. This gives you an opportunity to discuss your financial goals and current priorities without risk, and it gives the planner the opportunity to assess whether he or she can help you achieve your goals. At the end of the first meeting, you may decide that the planner is someone you can trust, is affordable, and that you want to hire him or her. Or, you may decide that this planner is not a good fit for you and move on. There's no obligation.

A financial planner helps you make the most of what you have, using strategies that are appropriate for your circumstances, goals, and individual tolerance for risk. He or she also helps you to get from point A (where you are right now) to point B (your retirement, for example) in the most efficient and reliable way.

It's important to understand that one of the key elements in successful financial planning is to keep your plan on track through personal challenges, alterations in the tax laws, and fluctuations in the market. It's not just a one-shot deal, where you receive your financial plan and say goodbye. Your planner should meet with you at least once a year to assess any life changes that have taken place and to make sure that you're hitting the milestones along the way. A good planner will act as a coach to start you in the right direction, and then follow up to ensure that you achieve each goal, step by step. There's nothing like meeting with your financial planner to motivate you to finally take action on serious decisions that have been hanging over your head.

One advantage to following a plan is that you can solve problems before they become crises. A retirement study by TIAA-CREF Institute found that people who planned more thoroughly for their retirement experienced far fewer financial "surprises" when they actually retired.

John L. Beckley, founder of The Economics Press, has become famous for his quote, "People don't plan to fail. They just fail to plan." Don't let inertia, bad experiences, or fear stand in the way of taking charge of your life. Comprehensive planning is one of the most effective steps towards achieving your retirement goals.

CHAPTER 3

WORKING WITH YOUR SPOUSE TO ACHIEVE YOUR RETIREMENT GOALS

———————

There are many times when we schedule an appointment with a couple, and when the appointment time comes around, only the husband shows up.

We ask, "Where's your wife?" Usually the answer is something like, "Oh, she didn't want to come. She thinks discussions about money are boring, and anyway, I make all the financial decisions for the family."

In the Japanese American community there are quite a few men who are engineers married to women who are teachers. An engineer has many enviable skills. He works with numbers all day and loves it! Not only that, he uses his keen analytical mind to make decisions to evaluate which path will ensure the success of his project. When he comes home at night to his educator wife, and there are financial decisions to be made, guess who does all the research and evaluation?

It would seem natural to this couple that the husband shows up for the meeting with the financial planner. However, when it comes to retirement planning, it's important for both spouses to attend the meetings and be involved in the dis-

17

cussion. The reason is that <u>retirement planning is not really about money</u>. The decision about how to deploy assets and money comes later on. First and foremost, retirement planning is a discussion about what's important to you and your family, what your priorities are in life, what goals you want to accomplish during your lifetime, financial and otherwise, and what sort of lifestyle you want to achieve in retirement.

The wife may not have an interest in discussing investing strategies, but she certainly has an opinion about what's important to her and the family, and she probably lets everyone know what her priorities are. She knows what her goals are, and what lifestyle she wants to enjoy. That's why we want her there at the meeting. Any discussion that takes place about these core issues without her input is meaningless.

The other reason that we want to involve the wife is because the financial planner and the husband can get together and make all the decisions they want, but who has veto power? It's the wife who is frequently the real powerhouse in the family. Naturally, we want to involve her in the discussion as early as possible.

Retirement planning begins with values, and everything flows from there. We've found that the spouse who has given the most thought to what's important and has the most clearly defined opinions about the direction of the family is not always the one who speaks first or the loudest. Consequently, we sometimes interrupt the spouse who starts talking and say, "I've learned that it's helpful to start with the spouse who doesn't volunteer first. Do you mind if we come back to you?"

One engineer explained to me, "I'm doing fine with my investments and other financial matters, and in fact I like doing it myself." This made us wonder why he had come in to see us. He said, "I know that someday, I'm not going to be around. My wife doesn't like dealing with the finances, and I don't want to leave her having to do it alone after I'm gone. So I'm shopping around for a financial advisor who understands my investment philosophy and is someone that we both like and trust."

Financial planning begins and ends with caring about other people.

CHAPTER 4

WOMEN & MONEY

E arlier, we explained that we wrote this book because we felt that Japanese Americans were underserved and misdirected by the financial services industry. This is doubly true for Japanese American women.

Women face different financial realities than men for a variety of reasons. For our older clients, it may be because women historically have earned less than men for the same work, resulting in smaller retirement accounts and less Social Security income in retirement. Additionally, some women took time off from work to raise children or they may have been hard-working home makers. At the same time, their financial needs and responsibilities were often equal to or greater than men.

MORE WOMEN ARE INDEPENDENT AND ON THEIR OWN

Times are changing, and that has brought about variances in the typical household structure. In many families the woman is now the main bread-winner, the business-owner or the head of household. These new realities are important to consider when helping women capture their financial goals.

A 2007 census by the New York Times noted that in today's society, for the first time ever, more women are living without a spouse than with one. Women are waiting longer to get married, are living with a partner but not marrying, are staying single after divorce, or outliving their spouses.

A significant number of women living on their own are widows. Women tend to live longer than men, some outliving their spouses by many years. Akemi's grandparents are a classic example of the statistical norms. On both her father and mother's sides, her grandfathers have passed away but her grandmothers are the epitome of good health.

 We call her grandmother on her mother's side "Goggie" because her first grandchild gave her that nickname and it stuck. Goggie is the strongest woman Akemi has ever known, aside from her own mother. "Pop," Goggie's late husband, passed away at age 75. Goggie, however, turned 88 this past July in great health, and has only been hospitalized once in the last 30 years. She is the first one up in the morning, brewing coffee, gardening in the afternoon, cooking dinner in the evening and folding laundry in front of the TV at night. When she fell and broke her hip, it was stunning to the whole family because she seemed invincible in their minds.

Luckily, she bounced back quickly, but not everyone is as fortunate. The fall is a stark reminder that while the surviving spouse may be healthier and therefore account for a longer life, they likely will require more care in their later ages.

Hospital stays, physical therapy and in-home nursing care can create a daunting pile of medical bills quickly. With medical costs rising at astronomical rates and insurance carriers offering less and less in coverage benefits, the importance of Long Term Care protection for women is more critical than ever.

It's not just in their later years that women are on their own. The average age of widows is just 55 years old. Many women are not prepared to be the primary decision maker at such an early age. The idea of managing the finances and creating financial direction can be frightening and can push some women into a state of immobility.

Women have the income, education, and skills that would enable them to make good decisions on any issue. However, decisions involving money can be intimidating because one bad choice can have rippling effects that are long-lasting.

Half of women surveyed by the Allianz 2013 Money, Women & Power Study said they are equally responsible for the major financial decisions made in their household. However, many of these same women felt they are not qualified to make knowledgeable financial conclusions. Although they tended to have a great deal of financial ability, they did not always have an equivalent amount of financial confidence.

The fact that most women will be single at some point during their lifetimes has implications in terms of their ability to thrive and have enough money without the help of a partner or spouse. Our responsibility is to prepare women for the very real challenges they will face during their lifetimes.

For that reason, it is very important for women to have a sounding board to bounce ideas off of before they make major decisions. They need an advisor who listens, who cares about them and is a fiduciary, required to always act in their best interests without conflicts of interest (see chapter on "There Are Financial Advisors, & Then There Are Financial Advisors").

INVESTING FOR WOMEN

Generally, women invest differently than men, so the growth in population of single women has an impact on the way we structure the asset allocation for our clients. Women tend to be more conservative investors than men. Many prefer less volatility in their investments and are willing to sacrifice some of the upswing potential for peace of mind. That's perfectly fine and the conservative approach is especially appropriate for senior or elderly women.

However, being too risk averse can be detrimental for younger women. Saving the bulk of their money in bank accounts or CDs is very safe, but those investment vehicles won't provide the necessary growth and income to provide for retirement, especially if they live for longer than actuarially estimated.

The Social Security Department says that a woman who is 65 years old today can expect to live to age 86, on average. A man at the same age is expected to live to age 84. However, one in four of those 65 today will likely live to past 90, and one in ten past age 95! With women living longer, it is important that they seek investments with a measured amount of risk that will allow them to stretch their money to match their life expectancies.

THE MODERN DAY WOMAN

"That's nothing, you want to try juggling three kids and a full time job."

Modern day women are busier than ever before. Many women juggle work, children, extracurricular activities, housework, family finances, social commitments, staying healthy and everything else from A to Z. We have found many times that what may look like procrastination or inaction is actually emotional and/or mental exhaustion from juggling so many necessary and competing tasks. Women are masters of resilience, multi-tasking and budgeting, mostly without complaint. With so many balls in the air, one is bound to fall every now and then.

THE GAP BETWEEN THE PRESENT & THE FUTURE

The challenge of multi-tasking is often expressed in women's struggle to deal with planning for the future while they are immersed in taking care of current issues and problems. An interesting study was conducted by the investment company, LPL, on executive women. They found the following kept them awake at night:

- Having enough for retirement – 71%
- Juggling demands – 47%
- Immediate family needs – 28%
- Elderly family needs – 26%
- My business needs – 25%
- Quality of life for family – 24%
- Volunteer/charitable intentions – 19%

You might notice that aside from the first concern of having enough for retirement, the remaining items have to do with addressing immediate, not future needs. Women deal with so many pressing needs on a daily basis that there is a constant struggle between what they need to take care of right now and what they need to do for the future. It is no wonder that in the day-to-day chaos, personal financial planning can fall to the bottom of the priority list inadvertently, even though it's also the top item of concern in the survey.

THE SANDWICH GENERATION

The term "Sandwich Generation" has become so common Merriam-Webster even added it to their dictionary in 2006. Sandwich Generation refers to the group of people who are caring for their aging parents while supporting their children simultaneously. Both men and women play vital roles in caring for aging parents and growing children. However, in many families, it is not unusual for the eldest daughter to be the primary source of care to her parents and the primary caregiver to her own children at the same time.

Due to the Great Recession, this stress has become even greater with many older children graduating from college but having limited job opportunities available. As these "boomerang children" return home, it creates even greater financial stress on the caregivers in the sandwich generation. Some have referred to this as the Not-So-Empty-Nest syndrome.

The National Alliance for Cargiving (NAC) study in 2007 noted that one out of four families has a caregiving challenge. Additionally, one family in ten has an impaired adult or minor child. Seventy-five percent of the time, the caregiver is female. Forty-five percent of those needing care live with their caregiver and another forty-four percent live relatively close. The amount of care giving needed weekly averages around 35.4 hours – the equivalent of a full time job. Not surprising, most of the caregiving is unpaid.

HEART, HOME & CULTURE

It can be challenging to determine how to allocate your finances and time to be the most efficient and ultimately the fairest to all of your family, including yourself! However, through prioritization of your financial and social needs, you may be able to save and spend in a manner that is in line with your values and goals.

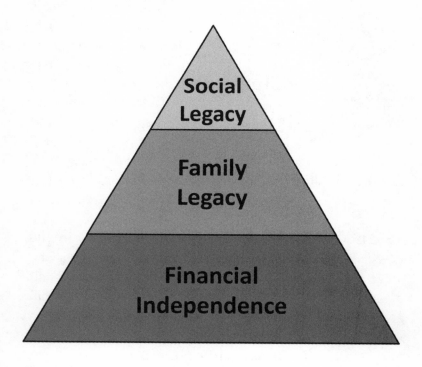

The planning pyramid above identifies three of the key focal points in financial planning. They are arranged by hierarchy, with the most crucial needs at the bottom.

Financial Independence (Heart)

Financial Independence consists of our basic necessities to live comfortably. At a fundamental level, this includes food, shelter, and clothing. In financial planning, we consider financial independence to encompass your desired lifestyle through retirement. It is important that you are able to continue a standard of living that promotes independence and meaningfulness throughout your life. Independence is at the heart of all our financial goals.

Family Legacy (Home)

After we are secure in our individual financial independence, we can focus on our family legacy. Family legacy includes passing assets to heirs in a tax efficient manner, but more importantly, includes imparting the next generation with the values and morals that you hope will guide them through their own lives. For example, in many households, education is esteemed as a cornerstone to personal development and a strong professional career. To support these values, you might set up a 529 College Savings Plan that will grow tax deferred, and may be used for qualified educational expenses, free of capital gains taxes.

For many, family legacy can be the never-ending bucket that people get stuck on if they don't leverage financial strategies to mitigate risks such as long term care for aging parents or college funding for growing children. Currently, long term care can cost a family about $94,000 per year and undergraduate college tuition can cost between $20,000-$70,000 per year, depending upon the university your child attends. If you have more than one parent needing care, children approaching college age, or a combination thereof, the annual costs can be astronomical, quickly depleting any savings you've accumulated.

We want to return to our parents the care and love they provided us for so many years. At the same time, we want to provide our children with an even fuller childhood than we experienced ourselves. Although well intentioned and admirable, it can be a daunting task if approached alone. For this reason, it is important to utilize your financial advisor to help anticipate your needs, find the best solutions and help achieve your long term goals.

> *"Other things may change us, but we start and end with the family." – Anthony Brandt*

Social Legacy (Culture)

Social Legacy can be the materialization of our hopes and dreams for our community. Many fall into the misconception that only the ultra-wealthy have enough to leave a social legacy, but there are tax savings strategies that can help anyone. You are really rerouting money that would have gone to the IRS in the form of taxes and instead giving it to community organizations you feel strongly about.

Japanese Americans have historically had close knit societies. They've made it a priority to take care of the organizations that preserve their community and further their values. It is great to see their generosity combined with modern day tax strategies that reward their philanthropy. We've committed a chapter to social legacy in Chapter 13, "Japanese Americans & Giving."

CREATING ORDER FROM CHAOS

A colleague compared financial planning to a jigsaw puzzle. Everyone has put together a puzzle on a rainy vacation day when you're forced to stay in. You lay out all the pieces on the table right side up and where do you begin? Many start with the corners or the outside border so you know the boundaries of the puzzle. We suggest that your first step should be to look back at the photo on the front of the box. What is the completed picture supposed to be – a windmill, a castle, four dogs at a poker table? It's really hard to put the puzzle together if you don't know what the end picture is supposed to look like.

Good financial advisors should want to understand their clients' definition of success and happiness, both today and in the future. Once they understand what their clients and their families want to achieve, they can help them put the right pieces together to create the end picture.

Completing the picture often involves dealing with what our clients need and want today versus what they will need and want in the future The job of the Certified Financial Planner™ is to build a bridge between the two and get them safely across.

THE POWER OF LISTENING

Because we are social animals, often the most important thing after food and shelter is to be heard. Women are accustomed to putting others first and being in a caretaking mode. Consequently, many have not been heard, and have put their dreams on hold. It's tempting for many well-meaning Certified Financial Planners™ to forge ahead with "making the plan work" by axing the vacation budget or other expenditures that seem to be less important than funding retirement or providing Long Term Care coverage. However, the family vacation may be critically important to the woman because it is an opportunity to bond with her family and adds meaning and joy to her life.

Advisors can understand what is important to women only by listening carefully to their stories and emotions, and encouraging them to tell us what matters in their lives. Financial advisors should not give recommendations until they are thoroughly engaged in the things that are important to their clients. They can then find ways to capture their clients' dreams by making adjustments in other parts of their lives.

A good indication that a financial advisor's office has made a commitment to women is if women fill prominent, professional and advisory positions, not just assistant and clerical positions.

Look for an Advocate

A woman should be able to view her advisor as her personal advocate. The advisor needs to be an advocate on two fronts – both for the woman that she is right now (and the goals and desires that she has currently) and for the person she will become (and the dreams that she will have in the future).

Not only must a financial advisor be able to tick and tie a financial spreadsheet, but they must also fight for the dreams and goals that make life worthwhile. Advisors draw from experience; both their own and that of their clients, to foresee what is coming down the road. They need to anticipate the day that their clients will become empty nesters, or provide for their grandchildren, or deal with the loss of a spouse. Whatever happens, an advisor creates value for their female clients by helping them understand, "I know what's coming, and I have your back."

CHAPTER 5

INVESTING FOR RETIREMENT

THE JAPANESE AMERICAN MILLIONAIRE

You would have a difficult time if someone challenged you to point out the Japanese Americans who are millionaires. It is not unusual to find them living in smallish houses in neighborhoods that have seen better days. They may be nursing along cars that are several years old, which they bought used to begin with.

Most of these Japanese American millionaires are not high-tech entrepreneurs or real estate moguls. We have met Japanese American millionaires who worked as gardeners all their lives. They made little and worked hard for every dollar, but they lived below their means and put away part of every paycheck. We have also been privileged to know Japanese American secretaries who were millionaires. They put $25 from every paycheck into their companies' stock savings plan, and the value of their investment grew through dividend reinvestment and stock splits.

Their financial success didn't come from a hot stock tip, a financial guru, or insider information. It came from discipline, good money-management and common sense. Yours can too.

FRUSTRATION

Many investors have had a frustrating experience when it came to investing. It seemed as though as soon as they bought a stock or mutual fund, it started going down in value. On the flip side, after they sold an investment it frequently increased in value. It almost felt like they were cursed with a Midas Touch in reverse – everything they touched turned from gold to lead.

The unfortunate conclusion that some people have drawn is that they should keep their money in the bank, under their mattress or in a coffee can in their back yard. One client's father told him, "If you want to double your money, fold it in half and put it in your pocket." However, this decision only guarantees that you lose earning power every year through inflation.

The good news is there are investment strategies that actually work. These approaches have been developed by economists studying the history of the market and the experiences of actual investors. Since your financial future hinges on your investment strategy, it's far better to utilize the best research and learn from the bitter trial and error of other investors than to risk your money making mistakes on your own.

Many of the errors made by the average investor are not really their fault. What you read in the media (in the financial press, on television and on the internet) can lead you to make assumptions about how the stock market works. These assumptions can sometimes direct you down the wrong path when making investment decisions. This is especially true because the financial media are so skillful at playing upon people's greed and fear.

There is a large and well-known mutual fund that did a long-term study of its investors. During a ten-year period, the fund had an average return of 17% per year. What was astonishing was that in that same ten-year period, 72% of the investors in that fund lost money. This seemed like a contradiction, but here is how it happened.

If you look at the long-term performance of the stock market, it's obvious that the market does well over time. On January 3 1950 the Dow Jones Industrial Average was 199. The closing price on January 3, 2013 was 13,391.

What is also obvious is that in the short-term, the market will either go up or down. The problem with most of the investors in the fund above is that they allowed the "noise" of the media to influence when they bought and when they sold. In other words, they became "noise investors."

When the value of the fund was increasing, the average investor heard positive things in the media about the great potential of the market or about this particular fund. When he or she finally decided to buy this fund, it was often at a time when the price was peaking. Right after the investor made the purchase, the value of the fund started to fall.

The typical investor held onto the fund for about a year and a half, hoping the market and the fund would turn around.

When the fund was close to bottoming out, the investor heard the doom-and-gloom stories in the media about the dismal future of the market or the poor prospects of this fund. Unable to sleep at night, he or she decided to cut their losses and sell. Because the investor bought high and sold low, he or she lost money. This is how 72% of the investors in the fund lost money. If they had held onto the fund, it would have averaged a 17% increase per year.

The point of the story is that there is a big difference between investment performance and investor performance. Even when long-term investment performance is good, many investors are sabotaged by their own emotions and "noise investor" behavior. Sadly, this is a common occurrence. The blame rests with the financial media for putting investors through an emotional roller coaster.

Who benefits from "noise investing"? It's certainly not the 72% of investors who lost money in the example above. The main beneficiary is the financial media. There are over 30 financial magazines, hundreds of financial television programs and thousands of financial "guru" websites competing for your attention. They need to sell magazines, advertising space and newsletter subscriptions. They know that one of the surest ways to ensure their own success is to trigger fear or greed.

One popular financial magazine sells a lot of copies by touting the "fund you should buy today" on the front cover. They make money by creating a frenzy about the latest hot fund or about the sizzling market. They make you anxious that you will be left behind if you don't buy right now.

Mutual fund companies also benefit from emotional investing. A large part of the compensation for fund portfolio managers comes from how much assets they have under their management. Therefore, portfolio managers benefit when their fund is promoted as the "hot fund" on the cover of a financial magazine, even if it's for only one issue. Assets come pouring in and the portfolio manager receives his bonus. Even if the fund ends up in the basement the next month, he's already accomplished what he set out to do. The goal of the portfolio manager is not the same as the goal of the investors in the fund.

Fund managers have a great incentive to do whatever they can to create short blips of good performance even if it is at the expense of healthy long-term performance. It helps the fund manager to send his children to college and to build his own retirement nest egg. What it does to the investor's retirement fund or children's college fund is secondary.

For the investor, it's not a good strategy to base your investment strategy on those short blips. The performance upon which you based your decision to buy a fund occurred in the past. It's like driving while looking in the rear view mirror. It doesn't tell you much about what's ahead of you, and chances are high that you will crash.

In order for a fund manager to create a momentary burst of good performance he has to do a lot of buying and selling. Many aggressive mutual funds have a turnover of 100% – 200%. This means that the stocks held by the fund at the beginning of the year can be entirely different from the stocks held by the end of the year. This generates brokerage charges, fees and commissions that are passed on to the shareholders of the fund. It also creates high, short-term capital gain taxes that are passed on to you. Even if an investor did no buying or selling personally, he or she could end up with a large 1099 tax bill at the end of the year.

Another phenomenon that trips up many investors is that conventional logic doesn't work when it comes to the market. The logic that helps you get through the day and make good decisions at work and at home can defeat you when it comes to investing. Most investors are very rational people, so they approach investing this way: "I want to go with winners, so I'm going to do my research and read *Money Magazine, The Wall Street Journal,* and my local paper's mutual fund report. I'm going to find the funds that did the best this year. Then I'll take my investment money, divide it among those great funds, and I'll probably do OK."

Unfortunately, this logical approach doesn't work in the stock market. If you put your money in the best performing mutual funds for the year, the probability is actually quite low that you will do well the following year.

This is because the market is made up of fifteen assets classes. They don't all go up and down together. Each has its day in the sun at a different time. The asset class that does the best this month is probably going to be replaced by another asset class that does the best next month. We'll explain more about asset classes a little later.

Investing in the stock market is one of the few ways that you can beat inflation and fund a comfortable retirement. The challenge is to create an investment strategy that will work for you. The way to start is to move away from being a "noise investor" and towards becoming an informed investor who understands how the market works.

RISK: TAKING THE LONG VIEW

The fear that keeps many people from investing in the stock market is the risk of losing what they invest. That's a possibility, because stock and bond investments are not guaranteed by the FDIC like savings accounts and Certificates of Deposits. It's the reason that investment professionals are required by law to tell you that, "Past performance is no guarantee of future results."

However, you are familiar with other types of risk, and you usually don't let risk paralyze your actions. When you step out the front door to go to work, there is the risk that you might get run over by a truck, but that doesn't make you stay in bed all day. Doing that would convert a potential risk to a real risk that you would lose your job.

When we talk about investment risk, what is the real nature of the risk? As we saw in the performance of the stock market since 1925, in the short term it goes up and down, but in the long term it keeps going up. The main risk, then, is for shorter periods, especially periods shorter than five years. These short-term fluctuations are the price you pay for the long-term gains. You can reduce, but not totally eliminate the short-term fluctuations. That's how the market works.

It makes sense, then, that if you are investing for the short term (five years or less), you should invest conservatively, perhaps in a money market fund or Certificate of Deposit, where the risk of loss is very low. You don't want to take the chance that the market will turn negative just at the time when you need to use your money.

However, if you plan to be invested for a longer time frame, you can afford to invest for more growth because the short term fluctuations are less likely to affect you. You will be farther up the curve, so that even if the market is up or down at the time, you will still be rewarded for your patience and discipline.

The most successful investors tend to be the ones who have the guts to stick to a long-term strategy. Most investors bail out too soon, usually at the first significant decline in the market. This is the consequence of "noise investing." Experienced investors have a more long-term view, and see a temporary decline as a buying opportunity. It's like going to shop at Macy's when there's a big sale going on. Someone asked John Templeton of Templeton Funds, "When is the best time to buy?" His answer was, "When everyone else is clamoring to sell."

PRINCIPAL RISK VS. PURCHASING POWER RISK

Taking a long-term approach to investing allows you to harness the true power of market growth by reducing Principal Risk and helping to overcome Purchasing Power Risk. Let us explain what we mean.

What would you guess is the greatest risk to your retirement lifestyle? The answer is Purchasing Power Risk. This is the danger that your money will buy fewer goods, such as food, shelter and energy, due to factors like inflation, government regulations, or natural disasters. A well-known measure of purchasing power is the Consumer Price Index, which tracks the prices consumers pay for goods and services over a fixed period of time. If we are going to be retired for 25 or 30 years, as the studies indicate, purchasing power risk becomes significant.

A prime example of reduced purchasing power is gasoline. A gallon of gas in 1982 cost $1.30 (remember the good old days?). Now it's as high as $4.25 per gallon. Since oil pricing is a black box and oil companies can pretty much write their own check, oil prices are not likely to come down any time soon. Gasoline has had a 227% increase over an approximate 30 year period.

The first class postage stamp is also a good barometer of inflation. In 1982 the first class stamp cost $0.18. Now the first class stamp is $0.48. We're looking at a 167% increase over about 30 years, but the Post Office still can't make a profit. Look for higher prices to continue.

Another way to think of Purchasing Power Risk is to think of your grandfather's salary. He probably worked hard to support the family and brought home a reasonable paycheck. However, you couldn't live off of his same salary today. You'd need to earn a much higher salary in order to have the same standard of living.

We know inflation averages about 4% per year. If you are losing 4% of purchasing power every year over 30 years, you can lose more than one-half of your purchasing power. Purchasing Power Risk is infinite.

There's not much we can do about Purchasing Power Risk except to invest our money in a strategy that grows our investment to meet or exceed the rate of inflation.

Principal Risk, however, behaves very differently from Purchasing Power Risk. Principal Risk is the danger that your investment value will decrease below your original investment amount. Principal Risk goes down over time and eventually goes to zero.

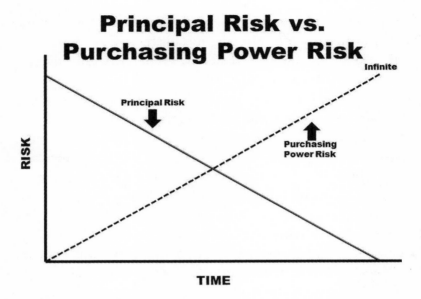

Principal Risk vs. Purchasing Power Risk

Here's why. The highest risk in investing exists in the short-term. Suppose you started a diversified portfolio balanced between stocks and bonds, and held it for only one year. Your risk of losing money over a one-year holding period is 23%. Those are not very good odds. This is why we recommend that money you need to use in the next one to three years (for example to replace your car or buy a new house) should not be invested in the stock market at all. You don't want to take the chance that the market takes a drop right before you're ready to make your purchase.

Over a longer period of time, the resilience and power of the market is impressive. When the Dow Jones Industrial Average hit a new record high in March 2013, more than doubling its 2009 lows, the Wall Street Journal's headline was, "Market Rewarded Those Who Stuck It Out." Only those who panicked and sold their investments near the bottom of the market were losers. In fact, since 1871 there have only been four trailing ten-year periods in which investors would have lost money in real, inflation-adjusted terms: 1908, 1929, the late 1960s and the late 1990s. The secret to harnessing the power of the market is broad, global diversification.

OVERCOMING FEAR

We know that the market gives good returns over time, but never goes up in a straight line. Therefore, you have to overcome your own feelings of fear when the market goes through its inevitable declines.

How do you overcome fear? There are three main ways. One antidote is to have enough cash in an emergency fund so you can outlast the down years. Even the worst recessions in our history have lasted only a few years. If you can ride it through you will generally be ok.

Aside from recessions, emergencies will come up regularly, often when they are least expected. You should have six months to a year of living expenses in liquid, stable accounts like savings accounts, money market funds or Certificates of Deposit. This will help give you more peace of mind and stave off panic during short-term downturns. Your liquid accounts can also carry you through most emergencies without having to liquidate any investments when they might be performing well.

Secondly, it helps to have a financial professional to talk to when you encounter the humps and bumps. Studies have shown that most investors who have no access to advice keep their investment only one and a half years. Since the most successful investors are those who plan their work, and work their plan, having someone to help you stick to your plan is essential.

The emotional "noise" that we hear from financial publications and television market commentaries often amplify the fear during market downturns. This can lead people to make drastic, irrational, investment decisions, and often results in buying high and selling low. A Certified Financial Planner™ can help you be more objective. When he or she gives you access to research and information, it allows you to see the bigger picture. When you understand what is happening, it helps to keep you on track towards your long-term goals.

The last element in overcoming fear is to have a well thought out, written investment plan. This is called an Investment Policy Statement. It's a blueprint that details your investment strategy. It explains why your portfolio is constructed the way it is, and how it's designed to meet your particular financial goals and risk tolerance.

When you meet periodically with your advisor to review your investment, it's comforting to be able to refer back to the Investment Policy Statement and see how you're doing compared to your goals. Before you entrust your life savings to an investment professional be sure to ask if they provide an Investment Policy Statement. It is an essential document.

If you are like most people, you want your investments to provide independence and dignity in your retirement. Perhaps your goal is to create a retirement income that you cannot outlive, an income that's rising even as your cost of living continues to rise. Maybe you want to create security for your children, or ensure the education of your grandchildren. These goals are at the core of your retirement and are interconnected. Employing the right investment strategy and working with a financial professional can make the difference in accomplishing all of them.

EVEN A BOOMING MARKET CARRIES RISKS

Greed and fear are flip sides of the same coin, and both can lead you off track from attaining your retirement goals. We mentioned the challenges you will face as an investor when the market is not doing well. When the market is booming your resolve will be tested as well.

In flourishing markets, fad investments tend to come out of the woodwork. They will solicit you by email, on television, by fax and by phone. If that doesn't get you, the media will draw your attention to this new offering that is beating the pants off every other type of investment.

Usually this fad investment will be concentrated in a particular industry or sector. The sales presentation will go something like this: "You should put your money in the new Biotechnology Fund (a fictitious name) before it's too late. You know what the average has been for this fund for the last couple of years? Seventy percent per year! Doesn't that sound attractive to you?"

When the pitch presents impressive performance figures, you should be skeptical and dig a little deeper. You may find that the numbers are correct, but that the salesperson left out a lot of the story.

Let's say the Biotechnology Fund had a phenomenal 220% return in its first year. Then, the following year it was down 80%. So, averaged over two years, the return was indeed 70%. Nevertheless, if you were an actual investor in the fund you would not have been happy.

After investing $100,000 in the fund, you would have been very pleased the first year. Your $100,000 would have grown to $320,000. However, the very next year, you lost 80% of that compounded value. The $320,000 would have fallen to only $64,000.

Your average rate of return was indeed 70% per year. You would have great bragging rights. Still, you would have lost $36,000 in real money. Always ask the question, "What was left in the portfolio?"

THE POWER OF DIVERSIFICATION

Diversification refers to a strategy of spreading your investments among different companies and asset classes. This helps to limit your losses in case negative events occur that might affect a particular market or industry.

For most investors, lack of diversification is a major weakness. It can be insidious because it's not readily apparent. You may think you're diversified because you have several different mutual funds and individual stocks, but in reality, you may have all your assets concentrated in one asset class.

When investors pick investments on their own, they tend to gravitate towards companies that are familiar names, like

Apple, Microsoft, General Motors or Proctor and Gamble. They don't realize that most of these companies all fall into the same asset class: large cap (that is, large capitalization).

Another common reason for lack of diversification is not knowing what companies you are invested in within your mutual funds. When we meet with a new client, one of the first things we do is a thorough analysis of the investments they currently hold. We've often see as much as a 50% over-lap in mutual fund holdings. For example, if you are invested in ten different mutual funds you might assume that you are well diversified. However, if the top ten holdings of each fund are the same companies, what you have is a very con-centrated and risky allocation heavily-weighted in ten com-panies. It's very close to putting all of your eggs in one basket.

Another danger in having a portfolio consisting mainly of large cap holdings is that the large cap growth asset class is only one of many asset classes. Sometimes, large cap invest-ments do very well. At other times, large cap is like an as-set class with a target on its back. When we went into the bottom of the Great Recession in 2008 and 2009, large cap U.S. investments were hammered the most. It was only after their accounts tumbled 50%-60% that many investors real-ized how undiversified they really were.

Having a diversified, rather than concentrated, portfolio tends to give you more protection during market downturns. If market performance moves from one asset class to another, you are ahead of the curve because you are already invested in the new "hot" asset class. The science of how much to put into each asset class is called asset allocation, with the most refined method being Modern Portfolio Theory.

CHAPTER 6

MODERN PORTFOLIO THEORY

M odern Portfolio Theory (MPT) was created in the 1970s at the University of Chicago by three econ-omists: Harry Markowitz, Merton Miller and William Sharpe. The three eventually won the Nobel Prize in Eco-nomics in 1990.

Modern Portfolio Theory helps investors avoid the trap of chasing performance. It is based on broad, global diversifica-tion and balancing the performance of different asset classes.

NON-FINANCIAL DIVERSIFICATION

Alan saw diversification in action in a non-financial setting when he and his wife went on vacation in New York City. This was during his wife's spring break, when she was an elementary school teacher. They travelled during a time of year in New York when the weather was unpredictable and changed quickly.

The subway station was conveniently close to their hotel and they used it daily to tour the city. Some days when they came up out of the subway to their hotel it was raining. Other days, it was a bright, sunny day.

Alan and his wife noticed on rainy days, a vendor would be set up at the top of the stairs, ready to sell them an umbrella when they stepped out into the rain. They learned later that many umbrella vendors are Senegalese who are famous for their ability to predict the weather. Even if it's a nice day, if you see a Senegalese umbrella vendor setting up his or her goods, be ready for rain – they know what's coming.

Then one day, Alan and his wife came up out of the subway and the weather had changed. It was a beautiful day. The sky was cobalt blue and the sun was warm and bright. There, at the top of the steps, was the same woman who had been selling umbrellas. This time, though, she was selling sunglasses!

They were impressed. The vendor has protected herself against the vagaries of the weather by carrying two product lines that were very different from one another! She had evened out the ups and downs in her income and created more security in her life.

FINANCIAL DIVERSIFICATION

Diversification in investments works in a very similar way. The following outlines a method of applying diversification to your portfolio. There are fifteen different asset classes – here are five of the major categories.

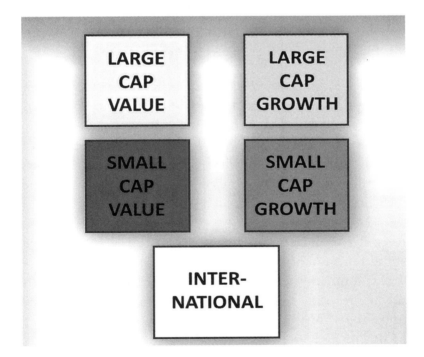

Different asset classes don't all go up or down at the same time. An investor can take advantage of this behavior by using many asset classes. They tend to balance each other out, reducing risk and volatility.

In the diagram above, you see large companies on the top horizontal row, and small companies on the next horizontal row. The up and down fortunes of large companies generally occur at different times from small companies. When large companies are doing really well, small companies often are not. We saw this in a dramatic fashion in 1998.

The opposite is also true. When small companies are doing very well, oftentimes large companies are having a hard time. During the 1970s, small cap (small capitalization companies) did significantly better than large cap. Therefore, if we have both large company and small company investments in our portfolios it helps to improve performance.

When large company growth stocks were the best performing asset class for several years in the mid-90s, many inexperienced investors were lulled into complacence and concluded, "Why don't I just put all my money into large company growth investments?" It's that, "driving while looking in the rear view mirror," behavior again. What was hot the last three years may be the worst indicator of what will be hot in the next three years.

A similar balance occurs between growth investments (the vertical column on the right) and value investments (the vertical column on the left). Growth investments do well when the market is booming and there is a lot of upward momentum. These investments take advantage of the momentum by buying high and selling higher.

Value investments are just the opposite. The value strategy is to look for bargains and to sell when the value recovers. Value investments do well when the market is down. They seek out fundamentally good companies that are out of favor at the time, not because they are bad companies, but because of circumstances beyond their control. One example would be just after September 11, 2011 when Disney stock and those of major airlines took a hit. They remained fundamentally good companies, but their short-term prospects were dimmed by the attack on the World Trade Center. It was a good time to buy their stock dirt-cheap. Over a long period of time, value strategies actually tend to out-perform growth strategies. Having both growth strategies and value strategies in your portfolio helps to reduce volatility.

Another balancing act occurs between U.S. investments (the top four boxes in the diagram above) and foreign investments (the bottom box). When the U.S. market is on a roll, the foreign market often lags behind. At other times in history, the foreign market has surged ahead when the U.S. market was in the doldrums. Whenever the U.S. market has been doing well for a few years, you may be tempted to put all your money into U.S. investments. Don't let it happen. The foreign market is too big to ignore. In 1969, US investments made up only 30% of total global investments. By 1997, this dropped to 21%. If you ignore foreign investments, you severely restrict your choices, lose opportunity and increase risk to your overall portfolio.

When you have all the asset classes balanced in your portfolio in the correct proportions, they can do marvelous things. They tend to give you more consistent performance, and at the same time help to reduce risk by tempering short-term fluctuations. Using Modern Portfolio Theory won't eliminate the oscillations entirely. That's the price we have to pay for the long-term gains. But when you reduce the volatility, you will likely be more comfortable with your investments and keep them longer.

HOW BALANCING ASSET CLASSES WORKS

After listening to this explanation of Modern Portfolio Theory one of our clients observed, "It sounds like if you have a highly-diversified portfolio, at any given time part of your portfolio is doing well and part of your portfolio isn't. Doesn't that mean you get no performance at all?" We have very smart clients.

We answered her question using the chart below. We mentioned that there are fifteen different asset classes. This chart uses just two asset classes, large companies and small companies, as an example of how balancing opposing asset classes helps to give more consistent and better returns.

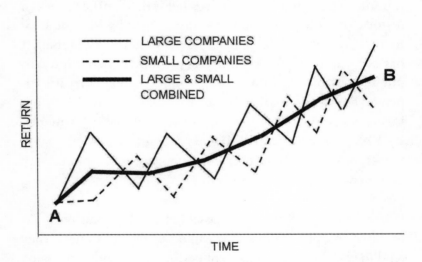

Large companies (represented by the thinner solid line) do well over time, getting from point A to point B. The problem getting from point A to point B is that it's like a roller coaster. Because we're human, it's natural to worry about the market and our investment in particular whenever they go into a slump. Our concern can get ramped up to panic when we turn on the news because the media is very effective at stirring up fear. When we're at the bottom of a market trough the pressure can be so great that we panic and sell all our investments just to put an end to the stress. The result is that we never get to point B.

The same thing occurs with small company investments (the dashed line). They do well over time as well, but we run into the same roller coaster effect. When small companies take a fall we can also be frightened into to selling at the bottom, never getting to point B.

However, if we put large companies and small companies together, they tend to cancel each other out in terms of volatility. When large companies are up, small companies tend to be down and vice versa. The net result is the fat, solid line on the chart.

Now, instead of a roller coaster we have fairly consistent performance from year to year. Because of the greater stability, we may be more at ease with our portfolio, and might sleep better at night. Most importantly, having a more consistently performing portfolio can give you greater confidence and makes it more likely that you will get to point B and accomplish your goals.

During market declines, if the drop in your portfolio isn't as bad as the Dow Jones Industrial Average or the Standard and Poor's 500 indices, the chances are better that you will hang in through the tough times. Modern Portfolio Theory helps you stick to your plan, which is 90% of the battle when it comes to successful investing.

CONSISTENT PERFORMANCE IS IMPORTANT

Reducing the volatility in your portfolio can also help your bottom-line performance. Here's an example. For simplicity's sake, we will ignore any trading charges, sales charges, taxes or penalties. Also, keep in mind that these returns are hypothetical and don't represent an actual investment.

BASIS	YR 1	YR 2	YR 3	END VALUE
$100,000	10%	10%	10%	$133,100
$100,000	20%	-10%	20%	$129,600

Let's say you have $100,000 in an investment that gives you a steady 10% return every year, compounded for three years. At the end of the three years you will have $133,100.

Compare this to another $100,000 in an investment that goes up and down. The first year it does 20%, and your money grows to $120,000. The second year it loses 10% and your value drops to $108,000. The third year it makes 20% again, so that at the end of the third year, you have $129,600. If you average the return of this investment over three years, it's 10% per year just like the first example. However, because it was more volatile, the actual net return is $3,500 less than the more consistent investment. This is another example of how average annual returns often don't tell the whole story.

Reducing the volatility in your portfolio using Modern Portfolio Theory has a couple of important benefits. You can be more comfortable with your investment, and your return may be enhanced. This is why large corporate investors and wealthy families have used Modern Portfolio Theory for decades. It just so happens that the MPT characteristics of more consistent growth and enhanced downside protection are what most of our clients want as well.

QUARTERLY REBALANCING CAN ENHANCE RETURNS

A key component of Modern Portfolio Theory is quarterly rebalancing. In investing, you always want to buy low and sell high. Quarterly rebalancing accomplishes this automatically.

We know from history that the best performing asset class often changes from year to year or month to month. No one can consistently predict next year's or next month's winning asset class.

Quarterly rebalancing helps to capture that performance without having to predict the future. It does this by imposing a discipline that an investor might not exercise on their own. If an investor owns a stock that is performing particularly well, he or she might be understandably reluctant to sell some of the holding, even if it makes sense to lock in part of the gains. This is similar to taking some of your winnings off the table in Vegas.

Modern Portfolio Theory uses regular rebalancing of the portfolio in order to sell high and buy low. Rebalancing uses the randomness of the market to its advantage. Suppose that Asset Class A has a good quarter and is up 5%. Asset Class B has a bad year and is just sitting there. Which asset class do you think has better odds of good performance next quarter – Asset Class A that just came off a good quarter or

Asset Class B that came off a bad quarter? It may be counterintuitive, but your better bet would probably be Asset Class B. When you rebalance, usually on a quarterly basis, you take some of the gain from Asset Class A and put it into Asset Class B.

The natural tendency is to hold onto a stock too long. Quarterly rebalancing gives us the push we need, forcing us to do the right thing at the right time.

THE DIFFERENCE BETWEEN MPT AND INDEXING

Some people believe that they can implement Modern Portfolio Theory using index funds. Index funds are a type of mutual fund that is constructed to replicate or track components of the market through common benchmarks. The most common indices include:

- Standard and Poor's 500 (S&P 500) Index – large U.S. companies
- Russell 2000 – small U.S. companies
- EAFE – foreign stocks in Europe, Australasia, and the Far East

However, index funds are not the same as asset class funds. Indices and index funds were created as marketing tools. For example, one large mutual fund company used to compare its fund performance to the Standard and Poor's 500 Index. When the company's fund performance started to look bad against the S&P 500, it switched to another index that suddenly made the funds appear to perform much better.

Asset class funds, on the other hand, are scientific tools designed specifically to be used in Modern Portfolio Theory. Because their mandate is to stay within the asset classes, they balance each other well and they have little or no overlap of holdings from one fund to another. There are several investment management companies that implement Modern Portfolio Theory as their specialty.

Many of these investment companies only accept investors who are working with a Certified Financial Planner™ or Registered Investment Advisor. They enforce this policy because they want investors who are informed and understand how the markets work, and are therefore less flighty. They have found that many investors who are not working with financial advisors tend to be driven by their emotions rather than by a plan. They rush to pull their investment out when they hear negative "noise," and rush to put their money back in when they hear positive "noise." This panicked buying and selling increases costs for all the other investors who are in the Modern Portfolio Theory program.

MODERN PORTFOLIO THEORY CAN REDUCE COSTS

Although Modern Portfolio Theory is one of the more sophisticated investment strategies, it can also be one of the least expensive. The savings come in the form of reduced annual expense charges when you use asset class funds. Asset class funds typically have very low expense charges. By comparison, the actively managed retail mutual funds that most people buy can have expense charges that are 2% per year or more.

Investments that use Modern Portfolio Theory usually have very low capital gain taxes and trading expenses. When you have a portfolio constructed using Modern Portfolio Theory, you could have more than 9,000 different companies represented in your investment. In effect, you are buying the whole market. Consequently, there is little need for much buying and selling except a measured amount when you do quarterly rebalancing.

Actively managed funds, on the other hand, buy and sell their holdings constantly inside the funds, increasing trading costs and capital gain tax liability. Even if you held onto the mutual fund and did no trading yourself, you could receive a large tax bill at the end of the year because of the portfolio manager's activity inside an actively-managed fund.

Many investment companies that use Modern Portfolio Theory employ a lower-cost fee-based structure, and don't impose any penalties if you should decide to terminate your investment. Your investment is liquid all the time. Therefore, you have much more flexibility and control compared to other investment methods. If your investment doesn't perform as you think it should, it's very easy for you to pull out and move on. This makes your financial advisor much more accountable to you. He or she has to watch your investment, keep you on track to meet your financial goals, and provide consistently good service if he or she wants to keep you as a client.

THE TORTOISE AND THE HARE

To be sure, there is a downside to Modern Portfolio Theory – it doesn't give you an adrenaline rush. Remember the race between the tortoise and the hare? When you use Modern Portfolio Theory, you're like the tortoise. The tortoise was not glamorous and had no impressive stories to tell over cocktails, but he won.

Whenever the market is doing well, there will be a trendy investment that is all the rage and will outperform your diversified portfolio. In other words, you as the tortoise are going to see the rabbit flying by. When that happens, you're going to be very tempted to lose sight of your goals, especially when the media jumps up and down and shouts, "Forget about diversification! This time it's different. Put all your money into this new investment now before it's too late!"

As we've seen in the past with tech stocks and real estate, just when everyone has piled into these investments the bottom can fall out, the champagne bubbles may burst and many people could get hurt. When it's your retirement account or an account your family is depending on, it hurts even worse.

Some people like the complexities of investing and enjoy the excitement of finding the next Apple or Microsoft, but don't want to jeopardize their family's security on their hunches. They can have it both ways. We often suggest they take 5% of their investable assets and play the market but invest their "serious money" prudently for their families using proven methods of diversification like Modern Portfolio Theory.

Your particular portfolio should reflect your unique investment horizon (that is, the span of time in which you will be investing), risk tolerance (the amount of up and down movement in your investment that you can tolerate), and financial goals.

EVOLUTION OF MODERN PORTFOLIO THEORY

Back in the 1970s, the first implementers of Modern Portfolio Theory were very wealthy families and large corporations. The reason was that when you put together a portfolio using Modern Portfolio Theory you had holdings in over 9,000 different companies, the broadest diversification you could physically get. At that time, you had to do it manually and purchase stocks in 9,000 different companies, requiring an investment of about $10,000,000 or more. The strategy worked well for wealthy families and large corporations but left average investors out in the cold.

Fortunately over time they were able to streamline Modern Portfolio Theory and make it more accessible. In the last few years, special mutual funds have been created that are designed as tools to be used within Modern Portfolio Theory, making it even easier for average investors to implement the strategy. Now you no longer need ten million dollars to use Modern Portfolio Theory. Regular investors can implement it just as effectively as the large ones.

HOW TO IMPLEMENT MODERN PORTFOLIO THEORY

Modern Portfolio Theory employs complex formulas, and requires an understanding of inverse correlations, efficient frontiers, standard deviations, Sharpe ratios and so on. Studying these, and keeping up with the constant market changes can be a full time job.

Our clients are very smart people, having established professional careers and successful businesses. If they devoted enough time and effort to managing their portfolio of investments, they could probably do it well.

Nonetheless, the last thing most of them want to do is to study optimization tables and asset allocation charts. They would rather travel, pursue their hobbies and spend time with their grandchildren.

The most efficient way for regular investors to apply Modern Portfolio Theory to their own investments is to work with a Certified Financial Planner™ (CFP) or Registered Investment Advisor (RIA). This doesn't mean that it will cost you more to invest. In fact, the opposite may be true. Many CFPs™ and RIAs manage investments on a fee basis, which is usually around 1% per year of assets under management. This means that they don't charge a commission or sales charge, which could be 6% or more on a commission-based investment.

WHAT TO DO WITH YOUR RETIREMENT ACCOUNTS WHEN YOU RETIRE

Most employees have no choice in selecting their 401(k) plan but must use the one that their employer chooses for them. Similarly, teachers or public employees who have 403(b) plans cannot move the money while they are still working. However, when you change jobs or retire from your company the window of opportunity opens and you can do an IRA Rollover.

Most employer-sponsored plans limit investment choices to a couple of dozen options. When you terminate, you can do a tax-free transfer from your 401(k), 403(b) or 457 plan into an IRA in which you have almost unlimited investment choices. Doing an IRA Rollover enables you to optimize your diversification and customize your retirement nest egg to your particular retirement goals and circumstances.

In June 2013 the documentary series "Frontline" revealed that 401(k)s are among the most expensive investments. Contributing to the high cost were fees that were unique to employer-sponsored plans. One of these was "revenue-sharing fees" paid to the 401(k) broker by mutual fund companies in order to be placed on the menu of investment choices. These fees were pocketed by the broker but the cost was passed on to the employees participating in the plan.

One of the common-sense rules in investing is that reducing fees almost always gives you better performance. Even if you chose the same investments, rolling from an expensive 401(k) to a lower cost IRA should be beneficial.

It is tax-free to roll over your employer-sponsored retirement plan to your IRA if you do it correctly. The rules can be complex and the IRS penalties can be severe if you make a mistake, so this is an area where it would be wise to consult a professional.

To summarize the benefits:
- Qualified rollovers from an employer-sponsored plan to an IRA are tax-free.

- The money continues to grow tax-deferred. In other words you won't receive a 1099 unless you take distributions.
- Employer-sponsored plans are some of the most expensive types of investments. If you can reduce fees by rolling over to an IRA it will help to give your investment better performance.
- IRAs can give you more direct control over your investment and offer more investment choices.

CHAPTER 7

REDUCING TAXES ON RETIREMENT INCOME

O ut of the following expense categories, which one would you guess is the biggest retirement expense?

- Clothing
- Food
- Transportation
- Medical Care
- Housing
- Taxes

If you guessed taxes you're absolutely right! Taxes eat up about 30% of the average retiree's monthly income, according to a 2011 study by the Employee Benefits Research Institute.

The IRS can impose heavy penalties as well. There are different penalties for different ages. For example, there is a penalty for taking money out of your IRA too soon. If you take an IRA distribution before age 59 ½ you will generally face a 10% excise tax on top of the regular taxation.

Then there is a penalty for taking out money too late. Once you turn age 70 ½ you must take an annual Required Minimum Distribution (RMD) from your IRA or be penalized 50% of what you should have taken out. The rules on annuity distributions are even more complicated.

One of the keys to not running out of money in retirement is to have your CFP™ create a Retirement Distribution Plan that minimizes taxes and avoids penalties.

LUMP SUM DISTRIBUTION OR LUMP SUM ROLLOVER?

When you retire and want to access money from your employer-sponsored retirement plan (like a 401k, 403b or 457 plan) you will have to fill out a form that asks you to check off one of two boxes:

☐ Lump Sum Distribution
☐ Lump Sum Rollover

They look similar but have vastly different consequences. If you check off Lump Sum Distribution, your employer is required to withhold 20% of your retirement account and send it to the IRS for taxes. You receive a check for the 80% that is left. The tax-deferred growth that you had in your retirement plan comes to an end. Then, at the end of the year, you will receive a 1099 tax bill for the total amount. In other words, you will be taxed on the whole amount.

If, instead, you check off Lump Sum Rollover, the money is transferred from your employer-sponsored plan to your Individual Retirement Account (IRA) with no tax at all and no 1099 at the end of the year. You are only taxed when you take distributions from the IRA. The rest of the money continues to grow tax-deferred.

The form can be complicated, and whatever choices you make can have lasting consequences for the rest of your life. A financial advisor can help you select the options that make the most sense for you. Some employee benefits departments do the whole transaction over the phone. This is convenient but can also have risks. If the employee benefits representative misunderstands you or makes a mistake, you have no independent documentation. Having your Certified Financial Planner™ on the conference call can give you valuable back-up if there is a communication lapse.

DON'T LET YOUR INVESTMENTS MAKE YOUR TAXES WORSE

In the section on Taxation of Social Security Benefits we point out that if your Provisional Income is too high, you can be taxed on as much as 85% of your Social Security benefits. On top of that, many people entering retirement find that they have to pay Quarterly Estimated Taxes for the first time. This wasn't the vision of carefree retirement that they expected.

Your current investments may be tipping you over the edge to higher taxation because they are generating taxable interest, taxable dividends and capital gains tax. You can reposition them instead into tax-free, tax-deferred, tax-credit and tax-managed strategies. This will help to reduce taxation of your Social Security benefits and might eliminate Quarterly Estimated Taxes.

PUT THE RIGHT INVESTMENTS IN THE RIGHT ACCOUNTS

Putting the right investment in the right account has the potential to both reduce your tax liability and give you better investment performance. In general, investments that are highly-taxed will do better in accounts that are tax-deferred, such as IRAs and 401(k)s. For example, a growth mutual fund that would normally trigger a great deal of capital gains taxes would flourish within an IRA or 401(k) where it can grow tax-deferred. Similarly, investments held less than a year would usually be taxed at high, ordinary income rates. Inside an IRA or 401(k) they also grow tax-deferred.

There are other types of investments that have lower tax liability, like dividend-oriented investments and tax-exempt municipal bonds. Investments held a year or more qualify for lower, long-term capital gains tax. These would do better in taxable accounts where they can take full advantage of their lower-tax status.

Making your money last for your lifetime is challenging enough without having the IRS nibble away at it. Cartoonist Bob Thaves of *Frank and Ernest* fame observed, "I don't know if I can live on my income or not – the government won't let me try it!"

CHAPTER 8

THE PROMISES &
PERILS OF ANNUITIES

We have devoted a chapter to annuities because they can be at the same time one of the most unique investments and one of the most hazardous.

Annuities are investment contracts created by insurance companies. They relate to life insurance in the sense that both have death benefits, but the emphasis of annuities is on growth rather than protection. What sets annuities apart is their option to create a stream of income guaranteed for a term of years (like ten years) or for a lifetime.

It seems like every time one of our clients' CDs matures, they are pressured by their bank to roll it into an annuity. Sometimes it's appropriate, but often it's not. Many times, the annuity offered by the bank is not very favorable to the customer but brings a lot of commission income to the bank. As a result, some financial writers warn their readers to stay away from all annuities. This is not good advice either.

Annuities will likely become more important in retirement planning as the distinctive features of annuities and the income needs of Baby Boomers intersect. Baby Boomers are retiring early and living longer. This means that they have to fund more years of retirement than any previous generation. If they want retirement income that doesn't end before they do, they will need a financial strategy that allows their retirement nest egg to grow in step with inflation and, at the same time, provide some protection from loss. They will also need a guaranteed stream of income. Some annuities have accumulation, safety and income features that fit well with these needs.

Annuities are not appropriate for some investors and an excellent choice for others, depending on their goals and circumstances. For some people, an annuity can serve a valuable role as part of their diversified portfolio.

An annuity can have the following benefits:
- Creates guaranteed income for life.
- Protects against a downturn in the stock market if you die. Because they are issued by life insurance companies, all annuities have a death benefit. For example, if you put $100,000 into an annuity and the value drops to $50,000 because of a downturn in the market and then you die, your beneficiaries will receive the $100,000 death benefit rather than the $50,000 actual value.
- Provides another investment for tax-deferred growth after you've maxed out your IRA or 401(k).

The biggest mistakes with annuities occur when they are used improperly, with persons and situations for which they are unsuitable. You should evaluate an annuity with the same standards that you would apply to any other investment. Ask yourself:
- How soon will I need to use this money?
- What do I want to use this money for?
- Am I comfortable with the amount of risk I am assuming?

- Is the potential return commensurate with the level of risk?
- Is the cost of the investment reasonable?
- Are there penalties for early withdrawal (called surrender charges in an annuity)? How large are they and how long do they last?

Annuities tend to be popular when interest rates are low and CD and money market investments no longer provide enough income. When CDs lower their interest rates, they force many retirees who depend on the interest to take a pay cut. Annuities are also attractive when the stock market is uncertain because they employ strategies for downside protection not offered by other investments.

Annuities are investment contracts with insurance companies. While CDs are guaranteed by the FDIC up to $100,000, annuities are guaranteed by the claims-paying ability of the insurance company. Consequently, it's important to pick an insurance company that is financially strong, with at least an A-rating from A.M. Best.

DEFERRED ANNUITIES

There are two general families of annuities: Deferred Annuities and Immediate Annuities. Deferred Annuities are designed to be an accumulation vehicle. That is, you put money into it either in a lump sum or on a regular basis, and then you let it grow so you can take a distribution of the money, plus growth, at a later date.

Within the family of Deferred Annuities, there are two siblings, the Fixed Deferred Annuity and the Variable Deferred Annuity.

Fixed Annuities

Fixed Annuities generally pay a slightly higher interest rate than CDs, which is one of the main reasons that many investors like them. When you compare Deferred Fixed Annuities, look carefully at the guarantee period. Some annuities guarantee a high interest rate only for the first year. You may be disappointed when the second and subsequent years give you a much lower return. Annuity salespeople are supposed to disclose this information, but sometimes they neglect to mention it. The better annuities guarantee the interest rate for a longer period of time.

Another reason that Fixed Annuities are attractive compared to CDs is that the money that you put into a Fixed Annuity grows tax-deferred. You won't be taxed annually like you do on your CD investments. When interest rates are low the skimpy return on your CD is diminished further by taxation. Fixed Annuities are sheltered from this IRS "haircut" so your money potentially grows faster. Typically, you would use a Deferred Annuity as a retirement savings vehicle, and start drawing the money out after age 59 ½.

On the negative side, the Fixed Annuity has a penalty for early withdrawal, known as a "surrender charge." Don't make the mistake of committing yourself to a surrender charge period that is longer than the guaranteed interest period. You might find that you are stuck with both lower interest rates if you stay in the annuity, and penalties if you leave. The ideal configuration is to have the guaranteed interest period match the surrender charge period. For example, if you purchase an annuity with a 5-year interest guarantee and a 5-year surrender charge, you know that when the guarantees end you are free to pull out the money and invest somewhere else without a penalty.

Always ask to see the details about the surrender charges before you purchase an annuity. Some annuity salespersons may forget to tell you unless you ask. Watch out for surrender charges that are much higher and last much longer than normal. These terms can tie up your money and keep you captive for many years.

What makes it confusing for the investor is that the annuity sale is sometimes a hidden agenda behind something else that you really want. For example, there are some companies that offer living trusts at a suspiciously low price. These "trust mills" are able to do this because the trusts they create are predominantly boilerplate generated by the software they use. The attorney or his assistant plugs in your name, personal information and beneficiaries with very little customization. The software does the rest.

The real action happens after the firm presents the living trust to you. The firm may quickly move to "financial planning" and pressure you to purchase one of their annuities. This is where they make most of their income. Don't be swayed by the line, "It's not costing you anything. We're paid by the annuity company." It's quite likely that you're paying a lot.

It's another example of, "You get what you pay for." When you shop around for financial services, the least expensive provider can very often end up costing you the most.

Variable Annuities

The other sibling in the Deferred Annuity family is the Variable Annuity. This type includes investments in subaccounts that are similar to mutual funds. You usually have the option of a safe, fixed account as one of the investment choices, but you also have a variety of investment subaccounts ranging from conservative to aggressive. They are called Variable Annuities because your return varies with the performance of the subaccounts that you choose.

Deferred Annuities are very useful if you have high income and want to maintain the same standard of living in retirement. If you're a highly compensated employee or business owner, you may not be able to put enough away for retirement even if you maximize the contributions into your 401(k) and IRAs every year.

The Variable Annuity allows you to set aside additional funds for retirement that will grow without being taxed annually. Unlike the contribution limits imposed on IRAs and qualified plans like 401(k)s there are no limits for Variable Annuities. In addition, the non-qualified Variable Annuity does not demand a Minimum Required Distribution after age 70 ½ like other retirement plans. You can let it grow as long as you like.

As an executive or company owner, you can use the Variable Annuity as your own personal retirement plan to supplement what you put into the 401(k). After you've maxed out your qualified plan and IRAs, you can still make unlimited additional contributions into an annuity.

Annuity Death Benefits

As we mentioned earlier, a standard feature of Deferred Annuities, whether they are fixed or variable, is the death benefit that is part of the policy. It's especially useful during periods when the stock market is volatile. If a Variable Annuity is temporarily down in value because of market conditions when the policyholder dies, the death benefit ensures that the beneficiaries get back as least as much as the original investment, minus any charges and previous withdrawals.

Over the years, companies have made the death benefit in the variable annuity more powerful. The original variable annuity only guaranteed that the beneficiary would receive at least as much as what the owner put into the annuity. Now, depending on the company, you may choose to have the death benefit ratchet up every seven years, or five years, or even annually as the market goes up and the annuity value increases, using an added-cost rider.

Having the safety net of the guaranteed death benefit can afford a certain amount of flexibility when it comes to investing. For example, a husband might employ a more growth-oriented strategy within a variable annuity than he normally would. He knows that his wife, the beneficiary, will receive no less than what he put into the investment should he die, even if the market goes down.

There is a cost for this death benefit. It's called a "Mortality and Expense" charge or "M&E." For most annuity contracts the M&E charge is about 1.25% per year. At what point does the tax-deferral advantage of the variable annuity make the cost of the death benefit worthwhile? It depends on the product, but the crossover usually occurs between seven and fifteen years. For this reason, a variable annuity would be more appropriate for someone who plans to hold the investment for ten years or longer.

Upside Growth & Downside Protection

Some of the new generation Variable Annuities have a second safety net called a "Living Benefit." During volatile market conditions, many people want an investment vehicle that will allow upside growth, but protect them on the downside. The Living Benefit is an added-cost rider that provides an income base that will grow at a guaranteed rate of return, for example 5%. The Living Benefit grows at the guaranteed rate no matter how your investment subaccounts perform. If your subaccounts (which are like mutual funds) outperform the Living Benefit, you get to keep all of the upside. If your subaccounts perform poorly, you can elect to take the Living Benefit value instead after a specified waiting period.

You should be aware that the Living Benefit value is not available as a lump sum, but may be converted to an income stream. Some companies require a ten-year waiting period as well. It's comforting to see the guaranteed growth of the Living Benefit on your statement during periods of market volatility.

Knowing what you should do is only half the battle. The short-term ups and downs of the market keep some people up at night and may cause them to make an emotional decision to sell. The Variable Annuity with the Living Benefit rider offers a way to participate in the potentially strong growth from equities while having additional downside protection. This may give some investors the reassurance they need to stick to their plan and not bail out of their investment prematurely.

Indexed Annuities

A recent variant of the fixed deferred annuity is the indexed annuity. The performance of the annuity is pegged to a stock index (usually the Standard and Poor's 500). The annuity salesperson's pitch for this type of annuity goes something like: "How would you like the kind of investment that gives you a safety net? If the market goes up, your investment goes up, but if the market goes down you are guaranteed not to lose any money."

So far so good. When we first heard this ourselves, we were intrigued. Why wouldn't everybody want this kind of investment? It sounded too good to be true. In fact it was.

The annuity salesperson told no lies. The value of the indexed annuity will go up if the market index goes up. If the index should go down, the worst that you could do is a zero return, not a loss. However, there was a lot left unsaid.

The annuity company limits the return that the policyholder receives in a couple of ways. The first is what is called a "participation rate." Let's say the annuity has an 80% participation rate to begin with. That means if the S&P 500 goes up 100 points, the annuity value goes up 80 points.

The problem occurs in the second or subsequent years. With most indexed annuities, the annuity company has the discretion to change the participation rate. I have seen the participation rate fall quickly to 50%, and then to 25%.

Another way that the annuity company limits returns is by the use of "caps." This is another term for a limit, or ceiling. For example, if the S&P 500 goes up 15% but your cap is 7%, your annuity will only receive 7%. This cap, too, can be changed at the discretion of the annuity company.

In addition, indexed annuities characteristically have a "surrender charge" or penalty-for-early-withdrawal that is higher and runs longer than other types of annuities. If you become unhappy with the structure or performance of your indexed annuity, it will be more painful to get out of it.

Because of the limitations imposed by the participation rate and cap, and because the annuity company retains the power to fundamentally change how the investment performs even after the policyholder has purchased it, we find it difficult to recommend this product to our clients.

IMMEDIATE ANNUITIES

The other family of annuities is Immediate Annuities. Immediate annuities are good at providing guaranteed income. The way it works is fairly straightforward. You put money into the annuity in a lump sum. Then the annuity company gives it back to you in regular installments that are guaranteed. As you can see, Deferred Annuities and Immediate Annuities have very different purposes.

Many people love Immediate Annuities because they don't have to worry about income. The type of annuity that gives you income for as long as you live is called a "Life Annuity." As an alternative, you can specify the number of years that you want to receive income. A "Ten Year Certain" annuity, for example, would pay you income for ten years and then stop. If you should die before ten years, the annuity would continue to pay the income to your beneficiaries until the ten years are completed. In between, there is the "Ten Year Certain and Life" annuity that would pay for a minimum of ten years, and then continue to pay as long as you live. If you are married, you might choose a "Joint and Survivor" annuity that pays over your own lifespan and that of your spouse.

Because the income is guaranteed, it is immune from the ups and downs of the stock market. Many people don't want to have to worry about their money in retirement. They don't want to guess at how much income they will be receiving each month because they have expenses that are fixed and must be paid no matter what.

Using an Immediate Annuity can also increase the income for some people. CDs, municipal bonds and Treasury Bills pay the same interest no matter how old you are. The income from an Immediate Annuity on the other hand will be higher for older ages. You may find that you can receive significantly higher guaranteed income from an Immediate Annuity than from other sources. The guarantee comes from the insurance company, so it's important to select a company that has a solid financial rating.

New & Improved

The old Immediate Annuities had a shortcoming. Once you deposited your money, the principal no longer belonged to you. It belonged to the insurance company. You exchanged the principal for a stream of income. It could also be scary because it was an irrevocable decision.

With the old-style Immediate Annuity, if you passed away early, the income stopped and the insurance company kept the balance of the principal. This made the older Immediate Annuities unattractive for people who wanted to retain control over the principle and pass remaining assets to their heirs.

The modern Immediate Annuities have better features. They offer a rider that allows you to get the unused remainder of your principal back at any time. This amount will also go to your heirs should you pass away. This is important if you should pass away prematurely and have only received limited benefit from the income stream.

Another shortcoming with the older Immediate Annuities was that the income payments remained level, while the cost of living inevitably increased. Over a long period of time, the owners found their purchasing power significantly reduced.

Some of the new Immediate Annuities still give you income for your entire lifetime and guarantee that the annuity payments will never drop below the initially scheduled payment. These annuities also provide upside potential, because they have subaccounts invested in stocks and bonds. Your income can increase when you have gains in investment performance.

Guaranteed income for life is more important now than ever before. People have taken great pains to eat right, exercise and see the doctor regularly to ensure a long life in good health. Ironically, many are now feeling very anxious because they fear living too long and running out of money during retirement. As life expectancy extends farther and farther, Immediate Annuities can be a valuable tool to provide guaranteed income for life, inflation protection, and liquidity for emergencies.

ANNUITY PERILS

Every investment has its own particular risks and negative potential. The annuity is no exception.

Tax Inefficiencies

Annuities can be great for assets that you plan to use during your lifetime. However, they are not very efficient for passing assets to children, grandchildren or other beneficiaries after you're gone, compared to stocks, bonds or mutual funds.

This is because stocks, bonds or mutual funds kept until death receive favorable tax treatment. They get a "step-up in basis" when they pass to your heirs. Let's say you purchased a mutual fund for $75,000 (your basis) and it grew to its current value of $100,000. If you cashed it out yourself, you would have to pay capital gains taxes on the $25,000 increase. However if your heirs receive your investment after you pass away, they benefit from a "step-up in basis" to the fair market value on the day you died, or $100,000. If they then sold it for $100,000 they would pay no capital gains tax at all.

Variable annuities, however, do not get a stepped-up cost basis when the owner dies. When the heirs receive an inherited variable annuity they must pay ordinary income taxes on the gain when they liquidate the investment. The tax that you owed doesn't go away but instead gets passed on to them.

Inappropriate Sales

Annuities have received a lot of bad press over the years, and much of it is justified. The abuses are particularly egregious when it comes to sales to seniors.

One client came to us after he had been scammed by some very aggressive "financial advisors." First, they bullied him into doing a new living trust even though he told them, "I already have a living trust." After they delivered the living trust they further pressured him into investing in an annuity. He reluctantly purchased the annuity by selling his stock. We did some research and found that the annuity company was being sued for $110 million by the California Attorney General's office.

Our client was stuck with a poor-performing annuity that had a penalty for early withdrawal that started at 12% and lasted for ten years. This client is in his mid-80s and he will not be free of these penalties until he is in his mid-90s.

If politeness can ever be a flaw, this may be one of the instances. Many Japanese Americans are extremely courteous and respectful to everyone and this client was no exception. The annuity sales people eventually wore him and his wife down.

What can you do to protect yourself? First, remind yourself, if it sounds too good to be true, it probably is. Then, follow these steps –

- Do not assume that just because a seminar or workshop is being held at a church, senior center or community center that it has the endorsement of that organization. Many scam operations use these facilities because they lend an air of legitimacy to their business.
- Do not be pressured into signing any documents on the spot. Legitimate financial advisors have your best interests at heart and are happy to give you time to think about and evaluate important financial decisions. If a salesperson will not let you take any documents home with you to study or get a second opinion, it should raise some warning flags.
- Ask the salesperson to sign and date a statement that summarizes his promises.
- Comparison-shop and get a second opinion from a respected financial professional like your accountant, attorney or Certified Financial Planner™.
- If you believe that you are the victim of a living trust mill / annuity scam, report it to your local district attorney or State Department of Insurance.

Complex & Rules Based

An annuity from one company can be similar to annuity from another company in outward appearance. Under the hood, however, the features can be very different, with numerous restrictions and penalties that may be hard to evaluate until you've purchased the annuity and put the rubber to the road. Annuity companies are continually competing against each other with new annuities as they adjust features and pricing. Because each annuity company is making up new rules as they go, it's challenging to compare one annuity to another and to know where to look for hidden traps.

This is why you should seek the advice of an advisor who is familiar with the annuity companies and their products and has enough years in the business to know how the annuities have performed in actual use. Frequently, abuses center around the annuity's "Living Benefit" option. The Living Benefit guarantees an annual interest rate (sometimes as high as 7%) on a secondary value that can be used later on to create a stream of income in retirement. What the annuity companies didn't count on was the steep decline of the market in 2008 and 2009. All of a sudden, their Living Benefit guarantee was incredibly generous and they were locked into it.

The plunge in interest rates made matters even worse. Annuity companies' usual practice was to gather all the premium money they collected and invest it in long term bonds. They hoped to earn a little more than what they had to pay out in distributions. With the drop in general interest rates, bonds abruptly dropped their interest rates as well, hammering annuity companies' bottom line. Consequently, annuity companies appear to be doing everything they can to slip out from under the liability of the Living Benefit feature that they created themselves. Many policyholders have found this out the hard way.

One annuity company had a Living Benefit that had to be exercised before the annuity owner's 85th birthday. One of their policyholders developed macular degeneration by the time he turned 85 and couldn't read the letter from the annuity company. He took no action and forfeited the opportunity to use the Living Benefit.

Another annuity company had a rule that if you took more than one distribution from the annuity, it would void the Living Benefit. One of their policyholders had their annuity in an IRA. When she turned 70 ½, she had to start taking annual Required Minimum Distributions (RMDs). She could have retained the Living Benefit if she had taken her RMDs from another IRA. However, the annuity company offered no advice, issued the Required Minimum Distributions and after two distributions, cancelled her Living Benefit rider.

Another annuity owner learned that his annuity was automatically annuitized to a stream of income. He realized this only after he started receiving monthly checks from the annuity company. He was starting to get dementia and didn't pay attention to the letter the annuity company had sent him. He found out that when he turned 85, the money in his annuity automatically converted to a stream of income unless he let the annuity company know ahead of time. The lump-sum that he had planned to use to pay for Long Term Care expenses was no longer available. The action taken unilaterally by the annuity company was irrevocable. His protests to the annuity company and the State Department of Insurance were of no avail.

A bank, insurance agent or investment broker will be happy to sell you an annuity. However because of the way they work, they tend not to give ongoing service and advice. Annuities, unfortunately, require continued vigilance because of their complexity, the IRS rules governing annuities, and because you cannot rely on the annuity company to be an advocate for you.

Exercise your own due diligence before you buy an annuity and work with a financial professional who you trust, is committed to long-term service and is required to always place your interests first.

CHAPTER 9

LIFE INSURANCE

No one has a crystal ball that will tell you when you're going to die, but you know that the event is 100% guaranteed. Although the possibility is probably remote that you will die anytime soon, if it should happen, it could be devastating to your family.

Life insurance is designed to protect you against that unlikely but very harmful possibility. The premium payment you make on an insurance policy shifts the risk of that event from you to the insurance company. Because insurance companies are able to spread their risk over a large number of policyholders, the cost to the policyholder is relatively low – you can buy thousands of dollars of coverage for pennies on the dollar. If anything should happen to you and you die prematurely, your family will receive an income tax-free benefit that they can use to complete the goals you had for them.

Japanese Americans care deeply about their families, and will make great personal sacrifices to protect them from harm and provide for their security. Life insurance is designed to take care of the loved ones who are left behind.

At the same time, not everyone needs life insurance. If you have been working for many years and are close to retirement, your children have probably graduated, are building their own careers and are on their own. They no longer need the protection of life insurance to self-complete their college funding. The mortgage on your house may be paid off, so you no longer need life insurance to protect your family's home if you should die. Thanks to the Fiscal Cliff agreement, the exclusion from estate tax has been increased and made permanent at $5,250,000 per person (indexed for inflation) so most people will not need life insurance to pay for estate taxes.

Life insurance still has its place if you want to provide tax-free cash and income for your spouse if you should pass away prematurely. It can deliver money to cover final expenses just when they are needed. Life insurance is also an excellent way to equalize an estate, for example when one child is active in the family business and the other child is not. The family business can continue under the ownership of the active child and the life insurance proceeds can go to the one who is not.

Those who have benefitted from a life insurance policy are quick to recognize its value. No widow, no matter how grief-stricken, has complained about receiving a tax-free check from the insurance company when her husband died. On the other hand, I hear many horror stories from those who suffered because their spouse or their parent suddenly died and left them with no resources and loads of debt.

Not long ago, a friend told us she was losing her house. "My husband died," she said. "He didn't have insurance, and now everything is going to hell." She was losing everything she had because she had no money to help her over this critical period. We think it's never going to happen to us, or perhaps we're just in denial. Thinking about the possibility of death is never pleasant, but it's usually better to face the risk squarely and take care of yourself and your family.

You can feel that your job is done when you have protected your family with life insurance, you have a diversified portfolio of good investments and your retirement plan is adequately funded. These goals can be your bottom line.

I often hear, "I'd rather put my money into investments." In reality, building an investment portfolio and having life insurance protection are sometimes both necessary, and one is not a substitute for the other. Building a portfolio will benefit you if you live. Life insurance may be necessary to protect your family if you die tomorrow.

The good news is, the cost of life insurance policies have come down steadily over the last few years. This is partly due to the competitive marketplace. Not too long ago, your only source for purchasing life insurance was a life insurance company. They had the entire market to themselves, and the high rates reflected it. The repeal of the Glass-Steagall Act, which maintained barriers between different types of financial institutions, suddenly made the marketplace for insurance very broad. You can now buy life insurance from the bank, from your stockbroker, or from the internet. The increased competition has driven down pricing dramatically to the benefit of the consumer. At the same time, people are living longer because of the increased awareness around proper diet and exercise. These improved mortality statistics have also reduced cost. Life insurance rates are now as low as we've ever seen.

When you're shopping for insurance, you should look for an insurance representative who is able to present many different companies to you, and is not captive to just one. He or she should have the freedom to work on your behalf to find the best company with the best rates. Insurance companies are constantly competing with each other with lower rates and better features to capture market share. The "cheapest company" pecking order changes from month to month.

The cost of a policy will be the same whether you buy it from an agent or from the internet, similar to buying an airline ticket from a travel agency or directly from the airline. However, if you have a good agent, he or she will be able to give you valuable advice, smooth out any bumps in the road during the approval process (called underwriting), and use his or her leverage with the life insurance company on your behalf if there are any disputes. Later on, when you need to make changes to your policy or file a claim, you'll have someone to talk to, rather than an 800 number.

Financially weak companies are more prone to raise premiums faster than stable companies. Worst of all, a weak company may be unable to pay out benefits just when you need them.

To a limited extent, states protect consumers against the collapse of an insurance company. State-run insurance commissions will step in and try to find healthier carriers to buy out a struggling company. If that fails, and the company goes bankrupt, states will pay benefits out of state guarantee pools funded by participant insurers. However, the benefit payouts may be delayed, and not all policyholders may receive the full benefits they are due.

To minimize the risk of your insurance company becoming insolvent, start by working with your Certified Financial Planner™. He or she can help identify the strongest carriers for you. Ratings often don't tell the whole story, so you should work with an advisor who is familiar with the claims-paying history of various companies.

The best policy for you may not always be the one with the cheapest price. Financially healthier companies often have higher premiums. Paying the higher cost may turn out to be a better choice in the long run than picking a cheaper but financial weaker company that could declare bankruptcy in the future.

You can look up the financial rating of an insurance company online or at the library. There are several independent rating agencies that compare all life insurance companies. The largest, most well-known rating agency is A.M. Best. The highest possible rating with A.M. Best is A++. In order to get a high rating, an insurance company must have more than adequate cash reserves, have a history of good claims paying ability, and hold its investments in very conservative instruments like highly-rated, investment-grade bonds. For safety's sake, you should choose only insurance companies that have a rating of A or better. Other well-respected rating agencies are Moody's, Standard and Poor's, and Weiss. Each agency has its own proprietary rating or grading system.

Healthy companies can become unhealthy, so you should review your insurance company's rating from time to time. If you see your insurance company being downgraded, it should warrant immediate investigation. There have been numerous cases where bankrupt carriers had been downgraded in the years shortly before going under.

HOW MUCH LIFE INSURANCE DO I NEED?

One of our clients shared a story with us about his father, who was a gardener. He passed away when our client was still a teenager. The family was not rich and in fact had many debts. The family's dream was to have the children go to college. His father had purchased a life insurance policy so the children would have the financial resources to get to college whether he was there or not. Our client said that if it wasn't for his father's policy, he would have had to go to work to pay off the debts and support the family. He might not have attained the professional career that he achieved. Now, with children of his own, he wanted to make sure that they were protected in the same way that his father protected him.

You probably have many hopes and dreams for your family. However, your life could be cut short by death or accident before those goals are reached. The odds for living may be in your favor, but if you're the one who dies, it doesn't really matter to your family what the odds were. Life insurance may be the last chance to finish the many great projects that you started for your family. The life insurance contract is a contract of time versus money – if you don't get the time, you get the money.

The question often comes up, "How much life insurance should I get?" There are two ways to do the calculation – the easy way, and the slightly more complicated way. Let's start with the easy way.

Life insurance is usually intended to replace your income if something should happen to you. You probably take a short vacation every year. What would happen if you took off forever? Your family would go on living, but with severely reduced income. How would your family survive? Start the calculation with your annual income, for example $50,000. Divide it by the rate of return you would expect from a moderate investment, perhaps 8%. The result is $625,000, which is what you might need in life insurance.

Here is what would happen if you had $625,000 in life insurance and you passed away. Your family would receive $625,000 tax-free from the life insurance company. Your family would then put it into an investment that is earning 8% per year. This investment would generate $50,000 per year to replace your salary without touching the principal. If your family encountered an emergency or needed a lump sum, for college funding for example, they could dip into the principal.

The slightly more complicated formula works like this. First figure out your immediate cash needs should you pass away. For example, these could include funeral expenses ($10,000), your mortgage balance ($100,000), an emergency fund ($25,000), and an education fund for your children ($150,000), which totals $285,000.

Then figure out the ongoing income needs that your family will encounter. Start with your annual salary ($50,000) and multiply it by the percentage that you would want to replace for your family (100%). Subtract from this amount any income that you may have from other sources, like rental income or investment income ($15,000). The net income need comes to $35,000. Divide this by the rate of return that you would expect from an investment (8%). This equals $437,500.

Add the totals together from the two previous paragraphs, and you get $722,500. This is approximately how much you should have in life insurance protection. Please be aware that these calculations, whether you are using the easy method or the more complicated method, are just a starting point. A good life insurance agent or Certified Financial Planner™ can help you customize a plan that takes into account your own personal goals and budget, and will help you arrive at the numbers and the type of policy that are the most accurate for you.

When you determine that your family needs the protection offered by life insurance, take action on your resolution and don't drag your feet. Good health is more fragile than many of us think. There have been too many times when a client has told me, "I'm interested in getting life insurance but I want to think about it. Can you get back to me in a couple of months?" When I follow up a couple of months later, I hear that he's had a stroke, or has been diagnosed with cancer. Today, you're insurable. Tomorrow, you may not be. If you're insurable today, take advantage of it.

ALL ABOUT TERM INSURANCE

When it comes to buying life insurance, an important decision is whether to buy term or permanent insurance. They are very different products and serve different purposes. For this reason, many people own both term and permanent life insurance policies.

Term insurance is designed to cover a specific, short-term risk. An example would be your home mortgage. Let's say you don't want your family to be left homeless if you pass away, and your 30-year mortgage is $200,000. You might get a term life insurance policy that has a premium guaranteed to stay level for 30 years and pays a benefit of $200,000 to your family if you should pass away. This would be called a "$200,000, 30-year level" policy.

When you purchased your home, you may have received a letter from your mortgage lender offering to sell you "mortgage insurance." Guess what? This is just term life insurance. However, there may be important differences in what your mortgage lender offers you, versus what you can get on your own.

The mortgage lender is capitalizing on an already-established relationship with you, and probably got his letter to you before the other life insurance companies learned about your home purchase. The mortgage lender's insurance is often more expensive than what you could purchase from your own agent. In addition, mortgage lenders often name themselves as the beneficiary of the policy so if you pass away, they receive the death benefit rather than your family. In other words, they're protecting themselves with your policy. If you got a policy on your own, you would probably name your spouse or other loved one as the beneficiary. That way, your family can decide what to do with the money, not the mortgage lender.

Another common use for term insurance is to ensure the college education of your children. You never know what the future holds, and it's possible that you could die before your children make it through college. A term life insurance policy is an inexpensive way to guarantee the money is there for them. To protect college funding a "15 or 20 year level" policy will probably do the job.

Remember that college costs are increasing at the rate of about 8% per year, double the rate of inflation. If current college costs are $25,000 per year, they could be $100,000 per year by the time your newborn grandchild reaches college age. To cover four years of college you might consider a "face amount" (that's death benefit in insurance lingo) of about $400,000 to get one child through college.

What do insurance companies look at when they evaluate you? They check your health, your financial stability, and your driving record. When you apply for life insurance, the company will ask you to take a medical exam, which they pay for.

Their medical company will come to visit you at your home or at work and will take 15 to 30 minutes to draw some blood, take a urine sample, take your blood pressure, and ask some questions about your medical history. They will also ask your doctor for a copy of your medical records, and ask the DMV for your driving record.

There is an important feature in term policies that's not readily apparent when you're simply comparing prices. That feature is called a "conversion" or the right to change from a term policy to a permanent policy. This would be important if you were in the 15th year of a "15-year level" term policy and you were just diagnosed with cancer. Now you need life insurance more than ever, but your term policy is coming to an end. What can you do? Because of the cancer, you would probably be declined if you applied for a new policy.

This is where the right to convert your old policy becomes very critical. If your policy is "convertible" you have the right to change from a term policy to a permanent policy without having to take another medical exam. Insurance companies vary greatly in their conversion rights. Some have restrictions on age, some have restrictions on how many years the conversion rights are available, and some have no conversion rights at all. A good insurance agent or Certified Financial Planner™ will know the differences and will be able to explain them to you.

Although term insurance is very inexpensive during the "level period" it's not designed to be kept longer than that. Beyond the level period the premium shoots up dramatically. Term insurance is the better choice for covering risks like the mortgage balance or college costs for the children. Once the mortgage is paid off or the children are graduated the need for insurance is gone and you can safely cancel the insurance policy.

PERMANENT INSURANCE

For people with longer-term insurance needs, permanent insurance is the better choice, and in many ways, a better deal. For this reason, permanent life insurance is more appropriate than term insurance for retirement and estate planning.

Permanent insurance is designed to be kept for life, in contrast to term insurance. You only have to take the medical exam once, when you apply for the policy. Even if your health declines over time, the insurance company is locked into keeping the policy going as long as you keep paying the premium.

With some permanent policies, the death benefit increases every year. This way, it keeps up with inflation or the increasing needs of your family. Permanent insurance can also be designed so that you can pay it off over a shorter period, thereby reducing total cost. This is similar to choosing a 15-year home mortgage over a 30-year mortgage.

If you should decide to cancel a life insurance policy in the future, what you will receive is very different between term insurance and permanent insurance. Term insurance works similar to car insurance. If you've had the policy for several years and then cancel, you don't get anything back. With permanent insurance, after you've had the policy for a few years, you will probably get some money back if you cancel. If you've had the policy for 20 years or more, the chances are good that you will receive close to what you contributed in premium. For this reason, many people feel that permanent insurance has better options and more flexibility than term insurance.

In order to accomplish this, permanent life insurance invests part of your premium in a side account called the "cash value." In the past, the IRS recognized the importance of permanent life insurance, and allowed this cash value to grow tax-deferred. People were attracted to this feature so much, they poured money into the cash values of early life insurance policies. Consequently, the IRS placed limits on the amount you can put into the cash value, ensuring that permanent policies serve their intended purpose as insurance rather than as an investment.

In many permanent life insurance policies, sufficient cash value will have accumulated after about 20 years, such that no further premium payments will be required. This is because the interest, returns or dividends are enough to cover the monthly cost of insurance. When this happens, the policy "runs on its own."

There are different types of permanent life insurance policies, depending on how the cash value is invested. The earliest type of permanent life insurance is Whole Life. If we were to compare it to an investment, it would be similar to a Certificate of Deposit in the sense that the insurance company would declare a rate of return which was usually quite low, but guaranteed by the company.

Consumers liked the safety of whole life policies, but weren't thrilled about the low return. That led to the next major development in permanent policies, Universal Life. These policies have a bottom-line, guaranteed interest, but usually pay a higher, current rate of return based on prevailing, competitive interest rates. In addition, there's more consumer-friendliness built into the policy. Policyholders can reduce payments or even skip payments for a time without losing their policies.

The most recent type of permanent life insurance policy is Variable Universal Life. With regular Universal Life, the life insurance company invests your cash value for you in conservative bonds. By comparison, Variable Universal Life invests the cash value in subaccounts that are similar to mutual funds. You direct the investment yourself by choosing the subaccounts.

Insurance companies like Variable Universal Life because they can pass on the investment risk to the policyholders. Many policyholders like Variable Universal Life because they have more direct control over the cash value and have the potential to make it grow.

The downside of Variable Universal Life is that the cash value also has the potential to lose value. Policyholders were made painfully aware of this during the bottom of the Great Recession in 2008 and 2009. Not only did their regular investments and retirement accounts fall in value, but their Variable Universal Life policies did as well. They often had to put additional money into their life insurance policies to keep them in force. Because of this risk, our preference is to keep investments and life insurance separate. Although Variable Universal Life has its place, especially for younger people, we feel that for older families more traditional life insurance is a safer way to go.

Variable policies tend to work better for younger families that need both life insurance and a way to invest. For example, if you have young children, you may want life insurance on yourself to protect their college funding. You may also want to start a mutual fund investment for their college education. With a Variable Universal Life policy you can accomplish both at the same time.

When you take money out of the policy for college funding, you can do it as a loan so it doesn't become a taxable event. Many Variable Universal Life policies allow this loan to be taken at "zero net interest." This means that the insurance company has to charge you interest to keep the IRS happy but at the same time will pay you an equal amount of interest as if the money were still in the cash value, so that the two cancel each other out.

After your children have completed college, you may want to continue the policy to fund your own retirement. At retirement you can again borrow money from the policy at "zero net interest" without triggering taxes.

When you pass away, your policy pays a death benefit. The loans that you took out for college funding and retirement are deducted from the death benefit, and your beneficiaries receive the net amount income tax free. You were able to pay for college, fund your retirement, and give a legacy to your family all through one policy. Because of this flexibility and multiple uses, Variable Universal Life is sometimes called the "Swiss Army Knife" of insurance policies.

The risk with Variable Universal Life is that it works best when you keep the policy your entire life and die with the policy still in force. If you terminate the policy before you pass away, there is no tax-free death benefit to pay off the loans that you took from the cash value. You could end up owing money to the life insurance company and paying taxes as well.

Permanent life insurance can be used as part of your estate planning as well. If you were financially successful during your lifetime, your family may be liable for estate taxes when you and your spouse pass away. Your life policy can be configured in such a way that the death benefit remains out of your estate but is available to pay any estate taxes. This way, your heirs receive your estate intact.

Today, you have more choices in life insurance than ever before. Whether your protection need is short-term or long-term, whether your investment style is conservative, moderate or aggressive, there is a type of life insurance that is right for you.

CHAPTER 10

LONG TERM CARE: THE MISSING LINK IN HEALTHCARE PLANNING

Japanese Americans tend to have long life expectancies. It's fortunate then, that Japanese American culture holds elderly people in high esteem for their wisdom, experience and many years of service to the community. In Japan, they even have a "Keirou-no-hi," or "Respect for the Aged Day" on September 15 to celebrate long life.

When Alan was growing up right after World War II, he lived in a house with his parents, his sister, three aunts, his uncle, and his grandparents. It was one of the happiest times of his life. His parents both worked, so he spent his toddler days with Baachan and Jiichan (grandma and grandpa) learning Japanese songs and folktales from Baachan and watching Jiichan play Go (Japanese checkers) with his friends.

When Jiichan came down with lung cancer, the immediate family banded together to provide care for him. There was always somebody in the home, and enough people to do it in shifts.

Today, reverence for older people remains as strong as ever but is challenged by the realities of a changing society. Extended families living together have become rarer. In our mobile society, it's common for children to live far away from their parents, sometimes on opposite coasts or other countries. Economic times have changed too, and it is now common for everyone in the family to have to work in order to survive financially.

Even Japanese American families often find that they have to pay someone to provide long term care since they can no longer give it directly themselves. Providing and paying for long term care has become a growing concern for baby boomers and their parents.

A study by AARP called "In the Middle" noted that Asian American families are exceptional in their commitment to care for older members of the family. Three-quarters of Asian American children said that they are expected to care for their parents, compared to one-half for other American groups. In addition, Asian American children typically tend to do more for their parents, with four out of ten children providing personal and financial assistance.

It's ironic that AARP's study also found that Asian American children are the least able of all groups to meet these high expectations. This is because Asian Americans have the smallest average family size of all the groups studied. As a result, the children are less able to share the burden with siblings.

The children are also likely to be highly-educated and working in demanding, high-paying careers. This means that it's more difficult for them to drop everything, put their careers on hold, and provide personal care for their parents.

Some of our clients have told us, "I don't need a Long Term Care policy. My children have said they will take care of me." We congratulate them on having loving, devoted children. Then we point out to them, "Having a Long Term Care policy, especially one that provides Home Care, will make it easier for your children to fulfill that commitment."

This is because a comprehensive Long Term Care policy enables the children to utilize Adult Daycare or Home Care so they can go to work or manage their businesses during the day and take care of their parents in the evening.

Baby boomers often discover that they are the "meat" in the "Sandwich Generation" caught between caring for their children who may still be dependent on them, and their parents who have suddenly become dependent.

Parents of baby boomers and baby boomers themselves are coming to an important realization. They thought they had all the bases covered. They have life insurance, car insurance, homeowners insurance and medical insurance but they forgot the missing link in retirement planning. They now realize the need for Long Term Care insurance to protect their families from the impact of catastrophic illness and extended custodial care.

In the snap of a finger we can go from perfect health to long-term incapacity. All it takes is a stroke or heart attack or cancer, or simply a bad fall.

When Alan's mother-in-law came down with cancer, he lost a good friend, and also learned some hard facts about our medical system. He found that her hospital-assigned social worker's primary function was assessing her ability to pay her hospital bills. It was also the social worker's job to get his mother-in-law out of the hospital as soon as possible and into a nursing facility so the hospital would no longer be financially responsible. He learned that Medicare only paid for a limited amount of long term care. He also learned how all-consuming it can be to care for a disabled loved one at home.

It would be a mistake to plan for retirement without educating yourself about long term care. It is most prudent to look at the options available when you have the most choices in front of you – which is usually long before you need it.

PAYING FOR LONG TERM CARE

Can you imagine your hard-earned retirement nest egg dollars being handed over to a nursing home to pay for your long term care? It's happened to many people.

Studies have shown the high likelihood that you will spend more in healthcare in the last few years of your life than you paid in costs during all the previous years of your life combined (New England Journal of Medicine). To make matters worse, the government-sponsored resources that you thought would provide long term care probably don't apply at all, or only provide care in a very limited way.

You may have thought that Medicare would pay for long term care. It does, but only for 20 days. It will pay part of the cost for an additional 80 days in combination with your Medicare supplement plan. Since the average length of time that people need long term care is approximately 3 years, the 100 days covered by Medicare is welcomed, but falls very short of most people's needs.

Your Medicare supplement plan can pay for long term care expenses for the limited amount of time mentioned above. However, since it is coordinated with Medicare, it too, will cut off after 100 days.

In other words, you may have some coverage for skilled nursing care for the first 100 days, but after that you're on your own and have to pay all costs yourself. In California the going rate in a skilled nursing facility is about $260 per day (California Partnership for Long Term Care). This translates to $7,800 per month, or $93,600 per year. For the average nursing home stay of three years, this means a cost of about $280,800. However, the average long term care need for cancer patients is even longer at five years, and for Alzheimer's patients eight years.

These numbers will probably rise because of a number of factors:
- The increasing cost of long term care exceeds the rate of inflation.
- There are fewer insurance companies issuing long term care insurance policies, so competition is reduced.
- Insurers have recognized that people are living longer than expected and that they have underpriced their policies.

Do you think you'll be able to dodge the bullet and not need long term care? We're sorry to say the odds are against you. The Federal Agency for Health Care Policy and Research reports that more than half the women and almost one-third of the men turning 65 will spend time in a nursing home before they die. For married couples, seven out of ten couples now reaching 65 can expect at least one partner to use a nursing home sometime before dying.

These statistics can only increase because as people exercise and eat more carefully they will live longer. It may be counterintuitive, but the healthier you are, the more likely it is that you will need more long term care than the average person. Your friends may die from sickness and injury but you will be so tough that you will survive. However, you will also need more long term care.

Compare this to other risks that are common in your life. The chance that your house will burn down is 1 in 1,200. The probability that you will total your car is 1 in 240. The possibility that you will need long term care is close to 50-50. Yet, in many households, families have home insurance and car insurance but no long term care insurance. You would be wise to learn the facts, do a little planning and make sure you're prepared. You might not be able to avoid long term care, but you can take measures to prevent long term care expenses from ravaging your family's finances.

SHOPPING FOR A LONG TERM CARE POLICY

One of our clients came through a particularly difficult time in her life. Her husband's kidneys failed, and the doctors felt he would die in a couple of months. Her husband was a big man, and he used a special large-size wheelchair so he could get around. His wife bravely took up the responsibility for moving him, bathing him, and feeding him as he got weaker and weaker. He was stronger than the doctors thought, and he hung on not for two months, but for two years. The wife who was healthy at first suffered a heart attack from the mental and physical strain of caring for her husband. For a while it became a toss-up who would die first.

The wife eventually recovered from her heart attack and her husband passed away. It was at that point that she decided to get the long term care insurance coverage for herself that her husband never had. "I never want my kids to have to go through what I did," she told me.

The desire not to be a burden on one's children or spouse is a main reason most people get long term care coverage. The other reason is to protect the family's finances.

You make independent decisions for yourself all your life. It's an important part of your character and self-reliance. However, you can probably foresee the day when you will lose that ability because of sickness, accidents or old age. A long term care policy is a way to make the decisions now that will ensure your long-term independence, even into the years that you may become incapacitated.

Long term care insurance is very customizable. It is bundled with a number of important features which can be selected or not, depending on your needs. Furthermore, almost every feature has a range of coverage that can be individually selected. This makes it possible to closely match everyone's requirements and budget to the right policy. This array of choices is the strength of long term care coverage and also its weakness. To the consumer, the many choices that have to be made in constructing a long term care policy can be bewildering.

You must also pick from more than 120 insurers that offer Long Term Care policies. There are significant differences in policy features from one company to the next. There are also wide differences in underwriting between companies. Underwriting is an insurance term that refers to the insurance company's approval process. Before a company will offer you a policy, it will review your doctor's records to make sure that you are in reasonable health. Because underwriting criteria vary from one insurer to another, one company may turn you down flat while another company may have no problem offering you a policy.

When shopping for a long term care policy, you should compare the offerings of several different companies. However, your financial advisor may not be at liberty to offer you the products of all available companies. The company that he or she selects for you may be the only one the agent is allowed to sell and may or may not be the best solution for your particular circumstances. More importantly, if that one company happens to reject your request for coverage, you might give up, assuming that all other companies will see you the same way. It's not true. Make sure your advisor is not restricted to presenting options from just one insurance company and has the freedom present the best options available in the market to you.

California Partnership Long Term Care Policies

California offers special Partnership long term care policies. The state has endorsed only a handful of insurance companies to participate in the program and has selected them based on financial strength and stability, good claims-paying history and willingness to meet the higher standards required by the Partnership.

The Partnership policies may only be offered by advisors who have taken a special long term care course, passed an exam, and been approved by the Partnership. Since the Partnership policies are considered by many specialists to represent the best of the breed, you may want to select an advisor who is licensed and authorized to present them to you.

As the name suggests, these special policies are a partnership between private insurers who offer the primary coverage, and the State of California who provides the Medi-Cal secondary coverage. Medi-Cal is called Medicaid in the other states. Medi-Cal Asset Protection is available only in California Partnership policies.

These policies are unique because they offer two safety nets instead of just one. When a policyholder needs Long Term Care, the insurance company pays out the policy benefits first. When the policy benefits are exhausted, the policyholder may then apply to Medi-Cal to continue long term care benefits.

Normally, it is very difficult to qualify for Medi-Cal benefits. If you have more than $2,000 in total assets you would be considered too rich and will be denied benefits. However, those who have California Partnership policies are granted special terms. They can keep the $2,000 in personal assets that Medi-Cal normally allows. Plus, for every dollar that the policy pays out in benefits, California will protect one dollar of additional assets. This way, you may be able to pass on more assets to your grandchildren and still qualify for Medi-Cal benefits.

Let's say you are a single person with a California Partnership Long Term Care policy that provides $270,000 in benefits. When you need Long Term Care, the insurance company first pays $270,000 in benefits. However, what if you use up the $270,000 in benefits and still need additional Long Term Care? You may then apply to Medi-Cal for a continuation of benefits.

The State of California will protect $270,000 of your assets (plus the $2,000 it normally does not count). If your total assets fall under that threshold you can qualify for Medi-Cal long term care benefits.

These protected assets will also be exempt from any claim the State of California may have against your estate should it try to recover Medi-Cal costs. As a plus, the personal residences of California Partnership LTC policyholders are 100% exempt from Medi-Cal no matter how much they may be worth.

In creating the California Partnership policies, the state involved consumer groups who made sure that the best features were included in the policies. Consequently, California Partnership policies include the following:
- Inflation protection, in which the policy benefits automatically increase by 5% per year
- Care coordinator who must be a licensed Registered Nurse, Gerontologist or MA in Social Welfare (non-Partnership policies have no requirement for care coordinators)
- Restrictions on premium increases

You should be aware that the Partnership policies function best when you plan to retire in the state in which they are issued. The initial benefit that the insurance company pays is usually good all over the United States, its territories and Canada, but the Medi-Cal (Medicaid) Asset Protection feature only applies within each state.

How Reparation Payments Affect
Medi-Cal Eligibility

Some Japanese Americans received reparation payments from the U.S. Department of Justice as compensation for being unjustly incarcerated in relocation camps during World War II. These awards of about $20,000 per person were granted by Congress after a decades-long struggle for restitution by the Japanese American community.

You should be aware that these reparation payments are excluded from being counted as part of your assets when applying for Medi-Cal benefits. Because many Medi-Cal caseworkers are unaware of the special status of the reparation payments, you should be prepared to show them an award letter from the government.

After 60 years, it is common for this document to have been lost or mislaid. If you cannot find your award letter, request a confirmation letter from:

> U.S. Department of Justice, Civil Rights Division
> 950 Pennsylvania Ave. NW
> c/o NALC Building, Room 411
> Washington, D.C. 20530.
> Phone: 202-514-0716

You will need to send a signed letter that includes your full name, your full name at time of payment, date of birth, Social Security number, and address.

Even if you are armed with this letter, you may find that some Medi-Cal workers still don't understand that the reparation payment is considered an exempt asset. Be prepared and print the three All Counties Welfare Director letters that pertain to the exemption. Go to www.dhs.ca.gov. and click on the Services link. Then click on Medi-Cal Information. Click on the following years and numbers and print out the letters: 2000, letter #00-14; 1990, letter #90-96; and 1989, letter #89-112.

Medi-Cal likes to see the reparations money in a distinct account separate from other assets. However, this ideal is not always achieved because of the passage of time and the inevitable commingling with other assets. You can help by identifying what savings account or investment received your reparations payment.

HOW LONG TERM CARE BENEFITS WORK

Today, family support is being replaced by long term care providers, either in a nursing facility or in the home. Long term care insurance policies have become an important part of retirement planning because paying for long term care out of your own pocket is prohibitively expensive. How do you pick a good long term care policy out of the dozens available? Here are some features to look for.

In a world of acronyms, here is another one to add to your list – ADLs. This stands for Activities of Daily Living. They are commonly used when talking about long term care policies, and are important because they determine what triggers the start of your long term care policy benefits. The Activities of Daily Living are: bathing without assistance; continence (controlling your bowel and bladder); dressing (being able to put on and take off your clothing yourself); eating (with utensils); toileting (being able to use a toilet or commode); and transferring (being able to change position, for example from lying down to standing up). Some policies also include ambulating (walking or getting around without canes, crutches or walker) as an Activity of Daily Living.

When you can't perform a number of these ADLs on your own without assistance, you are eligible for your policy benefits to start. Policies vary in the number of ADLs they include for consideration. They also differ in the number of ADLs that you are unable to perform in order for benefits to start. For example, a two out of six ADL requirement would be a better deal than three out of six. However, an Alzheimer's or Dementia diagnosis alone can automatically trigger benefits to start.

Most long term care insurance companies offer a Comprehensive long term care policy as one of the choices. This means that the policy pays for home care, intermediate facility care and skilled nursing facility care, and is the most flexible type of policy.

One of the first decisions to make in selecting a policy is how much Home Care benefit you would like to have. For example, if the skilled nursing facility benefit is $250 per day, you can usually choose a home care benefit that is 50% of that ($125 per day), 80% ($200 per day) or 100% ($250 per day). Because the insurance company knows that home care is probably the first type of long term care that you will use, the more home care you have in your contract the higher the premium is likely to be.

If you plan to use home care sparingly, and have a home care provider come in a few hours a day, the 50% option will probably suffice. However, if you want to have home care 24 hours a day, 7 days a week, the 100% option will probably be more appropriate. Some LTC insurers have a daily limit for what they will pay for home care and others have a monthly limit. Because people who use home care typically bunch the service into a few days per week rather than daily, a monthly limit is better for the policyholder.

Intermediate care is provided in a facility for those patients who are still fairly independent and can do a lot of their own. Some policies will pay only 50% to 70% for intermediate care, and it's not always apparent. Be cautious and read the contract carefully.

Good home care features are important because most people want to stay at home as long as possible. Most home care coverage will pay for skilled medical personnel to administer shots, and give physical therapy or respiratory therapy when needed. It will also pay for occupational therapy, services to help you with the Activities of Daily Living. The best policies will also provide homemaker services without added cost: someone to cook, clean, shop for you, and drive you around.

The better policies will provide the following features as part of the basic home care coverage: home modification (covering the cost of making your home safe for you, including grab bars, widening doorways to accommodate a wheelchair, ramps to go upstairs, etc.); therapeutic devices (this refers to hardware items needed in your home, like a hospital bed, wheelchair, respirator, and physical therapy equipment); medical alert system (installation of a medical communication system that will dial the phone for you in an emergency); and caregiver training (so your caregiver will know how to lift you and provide assistance without injuring themselves or you). Other policies may offer these features only as an added-cost rider or may not make them available at all.

An important decision is how much Maximum Daily Benefit to request. The daily cost of Long Term Care in most states is $260 currently, and that's a good starting point. However, you may want to choose a specific nursing facility because of their reputation and level of care. Ask about their rates and use that as your benchmark. Most policies will give you a choice in Maximum Daily Benefit, which can range from $100 to $500 per day. Some policies that are sold online or by mail may give you fewer choices or none at all.

Make sure that your Long Term Care policy includes an inflation rider. This feature increases the policy benefit annually in order to keep up with the growing cost of Long Term Care. This is very important to ensure that the benefit amount is still meaningful years down the road. Without it, there could be a growing gap between the actual cost of Long Term Care and benefit that the policy will provide. The average cost of Long Term Care is increasing annually at a rate greater than food, clothing or the Consumer Price Index. At 5% per year, the average cost would grow to $424 per day in only ten years. If your Long Term Care policy did not have an inflation rider, you would have to pay nearly $60,000 per year out of pocket for Long Term Care expenses over and above the benefits received from your policy.

If you have inflation protection, your policy benefit increases annually to keep pace with the rising costs of Long Term

Care but your premium is designed to remain level. This annual inflation increase is an optional, added-cost rider for most conventional Long Term Care policies, but is built-in as part of all California Partnership policies.

One of the most important considerations in choosing a long term care insurer is the prospect of future rate hikes. All long term care policies have one thing in common – the premiums are designed to stay level for life BUT the insurance company may petition the insurance commissioner to raise rates for a class of policyholders. This means that insurance companies have the right to increase your premiums in the future.

Some insurance companies routinely increase their rates every few years. Other companies have made a commitment to keep premiums the same for existing policyholders. It's probably better to choose a company that has a history of not raising rates.

The premiums for most basic long term care policies are non-recoverable. This is similar to the way that automobile insurance works. You pay your premium annually for coverage. If you need long term care the policy pays, but if you die and never use long term care you don't get your premiums back.

There are some hybrid policies that combine long term care coverage with life insurance. They have some unique advantages over traditional Long Term Care insurance. These policies either pay Long Term Care benefits to the owner or a life insurance death benefit to the beneficiaries or both. In a hypothetical example, suppose you paid total premiums of $100,000 on a hybrid policy that promised $250,000 of

Long Term Care benefits and a $250,000 life insurance death benefit. Then you had a fall and needed Long Term Care. You received $50,000 of Long Term Care benefits before your health took a turn for the worse and you passed away. Your policy would pay $200,000 (the life insurance death benefit minus the Long Term Care benefits already received) tax-free to your heirs. The life insurance death benefit keeps the money in the family and none of the premiums that you paid would have been wasted.

There are actually many more choices to be made to customize a policy to your particular circumstances and budget. You should compare not only the policy features, but also the rate history, financial stability and claims paying ability of the company. Therefore, we recommend that you seek the help of a financial professional who has extensive experience in Long Term Care. Above all, don't wait too long if you intend to apply for a policy. The younger you are, the cheaper the policy will be. If you drag your feet, your health could unexpectedly take a turn for the worse, and you might not qualify.

DON'T BET ON MEDI-CAL

Medicaid (Med-Cal in California) is a state-sponsored program that pays for medical care on a needs basis. This means that you must qualify for Medicaid by having low income and low assets, or by being blind or disabled. States determine the eligibility requirements and how much they will pay in Medicaid benefits. It is predominantly for those who have an immediate need for long term care.

Because many states are concerned about running out of money for Medi-Cal or Medicaid, they are quickly tightening the reins in two ways – by limiting how much they will pay and making it harder to qualify. The Kaiser Commission on Medicaid and the Uninsured reported that 19 states plan to reduce benefits, while 27 states are in the process of tightening the criteria for qualification.

If you are still healthy and alert, planning to use Medi-Cal in the distant future is a risky strategy. You could do everything in your power to qualify for Medi-Cal under the existing rules, but by the time you need long term care the qualifications could be much harder to meet. And if you do qualify for Medicaid, it may no longer provide the care that you expect and need.

Medi-Cal has many rules restricting transfer of assets, and may try to recapture assets after you have passed away. Medi-Cal is not free money – it is more like an interest-free loan. Many families realize this only after Medi-Cal sends them a lien on their parent's home after he or she passed away. Consult with a financial professional to find the long term care strategy that will work best for you.

Already, we can see the impact of reduced funding on those who are eligible for Medicaid. In California, the Medi-Cal Policy Institute reported that 56% of Medi-Cal recipients said they had difficulty finding a doctor who would accept them as patients. In urban counties, only 55% of doctors accept new Medi-Cal patients and the number is falling. The reason for this grim report is that Medi-Cal only pays 35%-60% of the doctor's customary fee. As Medi-Cal enrollment increases, and available services decline, there will be fewer resources to serve more people.

Federal laws governing Medicaid are also changing. Previously, one's personal residence was an exempt asset under Medicaid and was not counted in the formula to determine Medicaid eligibility even if it was a multimillion dollar home. The new laws changed that. Currently, home equity up to $760,000 (indexed for inflation annually) is exempt but equity in excess of that amount is counted.

Federal law also extended the "look-back period" from 30 months to 5 years. This means that if you transfer assets to other people in order to qualify for Medi-Cal, any assets that you transferred within the last five years would still be counted in the formula. We can expect more changes like this as Medicaid funding is further depleted.

A dangerous path in Long Term Care planning is to transfer all your assets to your children or other relatives and plan to have Medi-Cal pay for your Long Term Care expenses. A woman transferred all her assets to her daughter in order to qualify for Medi-Cal. Then, her daughter passed away without warning. Her daughter's ex-husband remarried and walked away with the mother's entire life savings, leaving her with no daughter and no money as well.

What implication does this have for your own health care and Long Term Care decisions? It means that you may not want to rely on Medi-Cal eligibility as a dependable way to pay for future Long Term Care expenses. Medi-Cal has no guarantees and you have little control over what happens in the next few years. Eligibility rules will likely be more limiting and benefits may be further reduced from their current levels.

Of course, if you need Long Term Care immediately and have no other recourse, it makes sense to use all available financial and legal strategies to qualify for Medi-Cal.

Medi-Cal eligibility is not a substitute for comprehensive financial planning. The high cost of Long Term Care is a risk that is real, and choosing what looks like an easy way out may only make matters worse. Your strategy for covering catastrophic healthcare should be integrated with the plan for your overall long-term family goals. There are many solutions to paying for Long Term Care expenses, and they include financial and legal methods that are tried and true. The best solution is an analysis designed to achieve your most important goals including covering long term care expenses, with the overall objective of giving you enduring peace of mind.

CHAPTER 11

HAPPY 65TH BIRTHDAY!
WHAT YOU NEED TO DO
BEFORE & AFTER

When Alan turned 65 it was a surprise. His mother was surprised too. "I can't believe I have a son who's 65!" she said. The fateful day crept upon him like a thief in the night as it probably will for you. You should know what to do ahead of time because you'll be there before you know it.

There are lots of rules, regulations, deadlines and penalties associated with Medicare, Social Security, IRAs and 401(k)s. Simply checking off the wrong box could irrevocably trigger taxes that could easily have been avoided, or you could end up with no medical coverage for months and a lifetime of penalties. After working this hard to climb the mountain, you don't want to stumble just when you're planting the flag.

SOCIAL SECURITY

A growing number of Americans have been forced to delay their planned retirement date due to job and savings losses suffered during the past five years. According to a 2010 survey by Towers Watson, 40% of U.S. workers said they have resolved to retire later due to concerns about outliving their savings and fears of rising health care costs.

Postponing retirement not only means working longer, but also delaying when you start collecting Social Security. Currently, workers can begin collecting Social Security as early as age 62 and as late as age 70. The longer you wait to start collecting, the higher your monthly payment will be.

Your Social Security monthly payment is based on your earnings history and the age at which you begin collecting compared with your normal retirement age. To get your own real-time retirement benefit see the Social Security Administration's website at www.socialsecurity.gov/estimator

The Retirement Estimator gives estimates based on your actual Social Security earnings record.

This normal retirement age depends on the year you were born:

Year Born	Normal Retirement Age
1937 or earlier	65
1938	65 and 2 months
1939	65 and 4 months
1940	65 and 6 months
1941	65 and 8 months
1942	65 and 10 months
1943-1954	66
1955	66 and 2 months
1956	66 and 4 months
1957	66 and 6 months
1958	66 and 8 months
1959	66 and 10 months
1960 or later	67

Those choosing to collect Social Security before their normal retirement age face a permanent reduction in monthly payments by as much as 30%. Nevertheless, many people start their Social Security benefits at age 62, the earliest possible opportunity. Some people need the income. Others might feel that Social Security is endangered and they want to receive benefits while the program still exists.

For those opting to delay collecting until after their normal retirement age, monthly payments increase by an amount that varies based on the year you were born. For each month you delay retirement past your normal retirement age, your monthly benefit will increase between 0.29% per month for someone born in 1925, to 0.67% for someone born after 1942.

Which is right for you will depend upon your financial situation as well as your anticipated life expectancy. Those people who are fortunate to have a good pension or substantial savings may want to delay awhile. Similarly, if you are in no hurry to retire you may want to continue working longer and collect later.

Those with a family history of longevity who expect to live longer than the average person stand to gain more by delaying. If you expect to survive beyond age 82, you might consider a delayed collection. If you think you are unlikely to survive beyond age 78, you may want to start collecting at age 62.

Whenever you decide to begin collecting, keep in mind that Social Security represents only 38% of the average retiree's income, according to the Social Security Administration.

This means that regardless of whether you collect Social Security sooner or later you will need to save and plan ahead.

WORKING WHILE RECEIVING SOCIAL SECURITY BENEFITS

Your Social Security benefit could be reduced if you receive employment income *before* you reach your Normal Retirement Age (see above). For 2013, if you are under your normal retirement age, you will lose $1 in benefits for each $2 you earn above the limit of $15,120. For example, a retiree under normal retirement age with earned income of $16,000 and a Social Security benefit of $1,000 per month would receive about $560 each month after a $440 reduction due to earnings.

In the year you reach Normal Retirement Age, the reduction is less—$1 in benefits for each $3 you earn above $40,080 in 2013.

Thankfully, once you reach your Normal Retirement Age the earnings test is waived. You may earn unlimited income without penalty. There is a calculator on the SSA website which will help you to understand how the earnings test would apply to you.

TAXATION OF SOCIAL SECURITY BENEFITS

After you are done with the Social Security Administration, you now emerge on the radar screen of the Internal Revenue Service. The IRS can tax your Social Security benefits if you have substantial additional income.

This is based on the IRS formula for Provisional Income – Adjusted Gross Income plus nontaxable interest (such as interest from tax-exempt bonds and income dividends from municipal bond mutual funds) plus 50% of your Social Security benefits.

The tax is on a sliding scale using a formula which you can find in IRS Publication 915. Generally, up to 50% of your benefits can be taxable. However, up to 85% of your benefits can be taxable if your Provisional Income benefit is more than $34,000 ($44,000 if you are married filing jointly)

MEDICARE

Medicare is made up of four major programs. Part A covers hospital stays. Part B covers doctors' fees. Part C is an HMO plan that bundles all your medical services. Part D covers prescription medicines. In addition, Medicare Supplement or Medigap policies help to pay for the costs not covered by A or B.

Most adults become eligible for Medicare on the first day of the month they turn age 65. Whether you need to sign up, and how to go about doing so, depends on the type of coverage you select and whether you are collecting Social Security benefits prior to becoming eligible for Medicare.

If you have not applied for Social Security benefits you should contact Social Security to sign up for Medicare even if you are still working. You can go to a Social Security office in person or enroll online.

MEDICARE PARTS A & B

Part A is basic hospital insurance. It pays for inpatient care in a hospital or skilled nursing facility (following a hospital stay), some home health care, and hospice care. Part A is premium-free for most people, but beneficiaries share costs through deductibles and co-insurance.

Part B helps to pay for medically necessary services such as doctor visits or outpatient care, ambulances, emergency rooms, tests and durable medical equipment (wheelchairs, hospital beds, etc.). Premiums for Part B will be deducted automatically from your Social Security check. If you have not yet started Social Security you will pay a monthly premium for Part B. It comes with an annual deductible plus a 20% co-pay.

If you are not receiving Social Security benefits, you will be required to sign up for Part A and Part B. You have a seven-month window to do this. It starts three months before you turn 65, includes the month of your birth, and ends three months afterward. To be on the safe side and avoid missing the deadline you should contact your local Social Security office three months in advance of your 65th birthday to start the process. You can enroll at medicare.gov or call 800-772-1213.

If you don't have medical coverage under your employer's group plan, it is extremely important to sign up for Medicare Part B during your initial enrollment period. If you fail to do so, you could be subject to a permanent penalty of 10% for each 12 month period that you could have had Medicare Part B but didn't take it. You will also have to wait for the next general enrollment period between January 1 and March 31.

If you are still receiving medical insurance from another provider (such as your employer or your spouse's employer), you can wait to sign up for Medicare. To avoid late enrollment penalties, you have to enroll during the eight-month period that begins during the month your employment ends or the group health coverage ends, whichever is first. To avoid a coverage gap, enroll in Medicare a month before your employer coverage ends.

Even if you have employer health insurance, it may be advisable to enroll in Medicare when you turn 65. Many employer-sponsored medical plans coordinate with Medicare and become secondary in order to reduce their costs. In other words, if you require medical services, Medicare pays first, and then the employer's plan kicks in to pay some of the costs that Medicare did not pick up. Be sure to talk to your Employee Benefits department before you enroll in Medicare. Your employer may have its own forms and procedures that you will have to follow.

After you've signed up for Medicare Part B you are entitled within the first 12 months to a one-time free check-up from a doctor who agrees to be paid directly by Medicare. The check-up includes a review of your health, vision, and blood pressure, as well as preventive care services and referrals for treatment. See www.medicare.gov/welcometomedicare/exam.html

Medicare Part C

Both Medicare Part C (Medicare Advantage) and Part D, which is prescription drug coverage, are provided by private insurers whose plans are approved by Medicare. Information on these providers is available on the Medicare Web site (www.medicare.gov).

You can sign up for Part C and Part D when you first become eligible for Medicare. You can also sign up between January 1 and March 31 or between November 15 and December 31 each year.

Medicare Part C or Medicare Advantage is offered by Health Maintenance Organizations (HMOs). You must first be enrolled in Medicare Parts A and B before you join a Medicare Advantage plan.

In return for receiving your Medicare benefits the plan combines all of your Plan A and Plan B benefits in a single package and may offer additional coverage such as vision, hearing, dental, and wellness programs. A Medicare Advantage plan generally includes drug coverage and covers many co-payments and deductibles as well.

You may be able to lower your total medical costs by using Medicare Advantage. The possible downside is that you'll have to use the HMO's network of doctors and hospitals for your care. You may have to learn the HMO's system in order to receive good service, but many patients are satisfied once they do.

MEDICARE PART D

Medicare Part D is coverage for prescription drugs. It is voluntary and available to all people with Medicare A or B or both, regardless of income level and resources, pre-existing conditions, or current prescription expenses.

In essence, the Medicare Part D plan is insurance provided by private companies. It is important that you comparison shop because the formulary (approved list of covered drugs) varies from plan to plan. You should check which plan approves the drugs you normally use. Another difference might be what pharmacies you can use. If you join a Part D plan and you use the plan's network of pharmacies you may be able to receive discounted prices on prescription drugs.

The Centers for Medicare and Medicaid Services (CMS) expects the average 2013 premium for Medicare Part D to be about $30 a month. Part D plans are allowed to charge deductibles of up to $325 in 2013 (that is, you pay the first $325). Once you meet the deductible, you may still have to pay copayments or coinsurance charges for covered drugs.

Some plans charge no deductibles but the premiums are higher. Some insurers require prior authorization before you can fill certain prescriptions, or limit how much medicine you can receive at one time. Some plans cuts costs by making you try lower-cost generic drugs before they will cover a more expensive brand-name drug. They call this "step therapy." Since everyone has different needs and uses various drugs, it pays to shop around.

Then there is the so-called "donut hole" in Medicare Part D. This refers to a gap in benefits when you reach a certain expenditure in covered drugs, $2,970 in 2013. Once you are in the donut hole you will be required to pay all costs even though you have Part D coverage. The pain is reduced a little by a gap discount of 52.5% off the cost of brand-name drugs and 21% off the cost of generic drugs. Some plans offer additional gap coverage at additional cost.

If you are not under Medicare Advantage (Part C), you may want to enroll in Medicare Part D at the same time you sign up for Parts A and B. If you fail to enroll in Medicare Part D when you are eligible, or go more than 63 days without prescription drug coverage, you could pay a penalty. The late enrollment fee is about 1% of your premium for each month you delay and you will pay it for as long as you stay in a Part D program. Your next open enrollment period would be November 15 through December 31 of each year. Even if you do not need many prescription drugs now, you may still want to consider joining in anticipation of future prescription drug needs.

MEDICARE SUPPLEMENT INSURANCE/MEDIGAP

Because of its many deductibles, copayments and coverage exclusions, Medicare pays only about half of your medical costs. As a result, many retirees supplement their Medicare coverage with Medigap plans (also known as Medicare Supplement plans) which are sold by private insurers. You must have Medicare Parts A and B to buy a supplement plan, which covers co-payments, deductibles and many other expenses that you would otherwise have to pay out-of-pocket.

These policies typically do not cover long-term care, vision care, dental care, hearing aids, eyeglasses, prescription drugs, and private-duty nursing. If you anticipate ongoing use of these services, you may need to obtain another form of insurance or pay out of pocket.

When you sign a contract for Medicare Supplement insurance, you usually permit the insurer to access your Medicare

Part B claim information directly from Medicare and to bill your health care providers directly. In certain instances, Medigap providers will manage claims for Medicare Part A as well.

THE MEDIGAP ENROLLMENT WINDOW

You are allowed only one guaranteed-issue period for your Medicare Supplement policy. You have six months after you enroll in Medicare Part B to buy any Medicare Supplement policy regardless of your health condition. During this period, an insurer cannot refuse to sell you a Medigap policy or impose a surcharge because of your health status or pre-existing conditions. After that, an insurer is allowed to reject you or charge you more.

Medigap policies cover only one individual. Even if you are married, husbands and wives need to purchase separate policies. A standard Medigap policy typically is guaranteed renewable, which means that as long as you continue paying premiums, an insurer cannot use your health status as a rationale for cancelling the policy.

You're 65th birthday will be a much happier one if you're prepared and know all the rules. More than any other birthday, the decisions you make on this event can affect the rest of your life.

CHAPTER 12

THE POWER OF MULTIGENERATIONAL PLANNING

O ver the next couple of decades we will be experiencing one of the most profound transfers of assets from one generation to another in U.S. history – from the parents of the Baby Boomers to the Baby Boomer generation.

Depending on the study, the amount of transfer is estimated to be $30 to $45 trillion, a staggering sum by any measure. The event can be a life-changing one for many families, providing new opportunities and opening doors that may have been closed before. Unfortunately, some families may lose much of their family treasure through careless errors, triggering penalties and taxation unnecessarily.

The difference is planning. Multigenerational planning has been practiced by wealthy American families for generations – in part, that's why they're wealthy. You don't have to be a multi-millionaire to employ these strategies yourself. It's just that most people have not heard of them, and their professional advisors may be unfamiliar with them as well.

Multigenerational planning makes more sense now than ever before. The recent passage of the Fiscal Cliff agreement made permanent a fairly generous exclusion from estate tax of $5,250,000 per person. In other words, you have to have net worth in excess of $5,250,000 to have liability for estate taxes. A married couple doubles this to $10,500,000. As a result, not too many people except the ultra-wealthy are too worried about estate taxes for the time being.

What remains a concern for most couples is to make the right decisions that will create security, stability and opportunity for themselves and for their children and grandchildren. Multigenerational planning is one of the best ways to make the right decisions.

There are lots of examples in history of good planning and lack of planning. Elvis Presley died with an estate of $10,165,434. However, he paid $7,374,635 in taxes, penalties and settlement costs. His heirs received only $2,790,799, a loss of 73%.

More recently, James Gandolfini of Sopranos fame passed away with an estate of $70 million. However, he is expected to lose about $30 million or 40% to estate taxes and settlement costs.

By contrast, the newspaper tycoon, William Hearst, died with an estate of $57,115,167 but his loss to taxes, penalties and settlement costs was only 6%. Hearst did better planning and had superior advice. It's apparent that it makes a big difference.

Multigenerational planning has many different benefits and goals, but here are some of the most important ones:
- Enhance the goals of both generations.
- Avoid hidden traps when passing assets between generations.
- Protect trans-generational assets from creditors, divorce and the IRS

- Use trusts and corporate structures to reduce taxes for both generations
- Take advantage of the longer investment horizon to boost returns

We will explain each of these in more detail. The benefits of multigenerational planning are like the concentric ripples expanding from a rock thrown into a pond. It helps the parents' generation make more confident decisions because they know their children are in sync with those decisions and are on board.

It benefits children and grandchildren by providing money for education, businesses and professions. It can be a resource for generations to come.

As a bonus, some of the most effective strategies work best when done in partnership with a non-profit organization, community organization, temple or church. These strategies can give income back to the donors, allow more assets to pass to the heirs, and help support valuable community and church programs. You can help your family at the same time that you help preserve the community.

HOW NOT TO DO MULTIGENERATIONAL PLANNING

We have seen some very bad decisions made with the best of intentions. Many of these have had to do with transferring assets from one generation to the next.

One mother owned her house valued at $630,000. She had paid about $30,000 for it many years ago and it had appreciated in value well. She had one son, and wanted to make sure that the house passed to him after she died. She wanted to avoid the cost and hassle of doing a will or trust so she added her son to the title of the house. The house was then held in joint tenancy with her son.

She didn't realize it at the time, but her action exposed her son to thousands of dollars in additional taxes.

In joint tenancy, the $30,000 basis (the original purchase cost) was split between the mom and son, so each owned $15,000. Similarly, the fair market value of $630,000 was split between them, $315,000 each.

When the mom passed away, her half of the house received a step-up in basis from $15,000 to $315,000. When the house was sold after her death, there were no capital gains taxes due on her half of the house because the basis was now the same as the fair market value.

The son, however, got no step-up in value on his half of the house because he was still living. When he sold the house he had to pay capital gains tax on $300,000 (the difference between $15,000 and $315,000). The federal capital gains tax was about $45,000 and state capital gains taxes added another $15,000.

The tragedy was that the mom could easily have given her son a 100% step-up in basis and he could have paid no capital gains taxes at all.

If she had kept the house titled in her name alone until she passed away, the house would have gone to her son just like she intended. However, he would have received a full step-up in basis from $30,000 to the fair market value of $630,000. When he then sold the house for $630,000 he would have paid no capital gains taxes.

SAVE ON PROPERTY TAX REASSESSMENT

Your community may have laws in place that exclude some properties from reassessment when they pass from parent to child or from grandparent to grandchild. What this means is that when a property transfers down from parents, their children or grandchildren can pay the same low property tax that the parents or grandparents did.

Los Angeles County residents are fortunate to have Proposition 58, which states that, "Real property transfers from parent to child or child to parent may be excluded from reassessment." This was followed by Proposition 193 which expanded the exclusion to cover transfers from grandparents to grandchildren.

There is no limit on the exclusion for a principal residence. You could have a multi-million dollar home, and the property tax would remain the same when it went to your children or grandchildren.

For properties other than the principal residence, there is a limit of $1,000,000 for individuals and $2,000,000 for married couples.

Luckily, properties held within a living trust enjoy the same exclusion. However, transfers to and from entities, such as a corporation or partnership, cannot use the exclusion.

You have to file the Homeowner's Exemption claim within three years of the transfer. Form OWN-88 is the Claim for Reassessment Exclusion for Transfer Between Parent and Child. Form OWN-143 is for transfers from Grandparent to Grandchild. Both of these forms can be requested at the Los Angeles County Assessor's Office (213-893-1239) or can be downloaded from their website: www.assessor.lacounty.gov

INHERIT AN IRA THE RIGHT WAY

Retirement assets for the typical American family now represent the largest single asset that they have. It has surpassed the equity that people have in their homes as the single largest asset.

Many people assume that once they start the Required Minimum Distribution from their IRAs at age 70 ½, the assets will quickly disappear. If they are managed properly, that doesn't have to be the case.

When you turn 70 ½ you are required to withdraw only about 4% of your total IRA value. This amount is recalculated each year by taking the value of the IRA on December 31st of the previous year and dividing it by a factor based on your age.

This means that if your IRA is earning 4% and you're taking out 4% per year, the value remains about the same. If your IRA is growing at better than 4% per year, it will likely increase in value for most of your lifetime even though you are taking annual Minimum Required Distributions. This gives you the opportunity to pass your IRA to your heirs at the end of your life.

When you pass away with money remaining in your IRA, the investment management company will call the beneficiaries you named and say, "You're the beneficiary of this IRA. What would you like us to do with the money?"

Many beneficiaries will not hesitate to say, "Send me the check!" This can be a major error. Your beneficiaries actually have two choices – they can receive a check, or they can move their portion of the IRA into a Beneficiary IRA.

If your beneficiaries say, "Send me the check!" they will receive the check promptly. They will be pleased until the end of the year when they receive a 1099 for the whole amount. The distribution from the IRA will be taxed as ordinary income, as if they earned extra income that year. Often the 1099 is so large that it pushes the beneficiary into a higher tax bracket and they end up paying higher taxes on all their income. To make matters worse, the tax-deferred growth that existed on their parents' IRA also comes to an end.

The problem is that many beneficiaries don't know they have a choice, and the IRA custodian is not in the business of giving advice. Nevertheless, the choice the beneficiaries make can have long-lasting consequences.

There was a case in Long Island, New York where the father of a family passed away with a large IRA worth $1.4 million. He was the last surviving spouse so the money went to his only daughter as beneficiary. She got the call from the IRA custodian and her response was, "Send me the check!"

The distribution from the father's IRA was taxed for both estate taxes and income taxes. This was when the exclusion from estate taxes was much lower than it is today. The daughter netted only $350,000 from the original $1.4 million.

If she had received her father's IRA into a Beneficiary IRA there would have been no income taxes due on the transfer. The money would have continued to grow tax-deferred, and the tax could have been spread out over the daughter's lifetime, instead of in a lump sum. Over her life expectancy she could have received $12.5 million from the IRA.

A Beneficiary IRA has to be titled correctly in order to satisfy the IRS. Let's say Kenji Tanaka is the father and Mary is his daughter. When Kenji passes away and his IRA goes to Mary as the beneficiary, she should title her Beneficiary IRA, "Kenji Tanaka IRA (deceased 7/21/2013) FBO Mary Tanaka, Beneficiary."

Notice that even though this is Mary's IRA, her father Kenji's name comes first, followed by his Date of Death. FBO means "For the Benefit Of." Mary's name comes at the end as the Beneficiary.

Children should be aware that a Beneficiary IRA is different from the IRA that they start on their own. If they transfer the money from their parent's IRA to their existing IRA the transfer could be disallowed and taxed. They have to open a separate Beneficiary IRA that is designed to accept their parent's IRA. If the parents are working with a Certified Financial Planner™, they may want to instruct their children to contact the planner first if they should pass away.

It sometimes happens that the parent worked for a large company in which he or she had a 401(k), 403(b) or 457 plan.

When they retired from their company, they left the money in the employer-sponsored plan, which many companies allow you to do. However, when the parent passed away, the child had problems moving the money from the employer-sponsored plan to their Beneficiary IRA. The rules are more complicated when the two accounts are not both IRAs:

- The transfer must be direct from trustee to trustee
- The transfer must take place by the end of the year following the year of death of the original IRA holder.
- The beneficiary must take a Required Minimum Distribution by the end of the year following the year of death of the original IRA holder.

If any of these rules are broken, the transfer could be fully-taxed.

In order to avoid missteps, the parents can do their children a favor by doing an IRA Rollover from their employer-sponsored plan to an IRA while they are still living. The IRA Rollover is a tax-free transfer, and the money will continue to grow tax-deferred in the IRA just as it did in the employer's plan. The difference is that when the parent passes away, transferring the money from their IRA to the child's Beneficiary IRA is much easier because they are both IRAs.

People who receive Beneficiary IRAs must take an annual Required Minimum Distribution even if they are younger than age 70 1/2, but the annual requirement can be as low as 1% to 2%, especially at younger ages.

A good way to open the discussion about IRA strategies with your Certified Financial Planner™ is to review the beneficiary elections on your employer-sponsored retirement plans and IRAs. He or she will help you to make sure that you have chosen the method that will make the most of these accounts over your lifetime and the life expectancies of your children and grandchildren. Retirement assets can be either one of the greatest legacies for your children and grandchildren or a tax time bomb, depending on whether you plan ahead. By using the correct IRA strategy, you can minimize distributions, keep more assets in your family and gain greater control over the assets than you had before.

THE ROTH IRA & MULTIGENERATIONAL PLANNING

The Roth IRA has the potential to give multigenerational planning a turbo boost. This is because the Roth has the following unique features:

- No Required Minimum Distributions are necessary with Roth IRAs. You can let all of the Roth continue to grow.
- The original Roth IRA can transfer to a Beneficiary Roth IRA without taxation.
- The Beneficiary Roth IRA continues to grow tax-free.
- Distributions from the Beneficiary Roth IRA are also tax-free.

When a Roth IRA starts and ends within one person's life expectancy, the growth advantages are significant but modest. When the Roth IRA is passed on to continue the compounding in the next generation the growth potential really blossoms.

As with any investment, the growth curve starts off shallow and then picks up speed over time. Towards the end, the curve goes almost vertical as capital gains, interest and dividends pile on and add to the investment return. With the Roth IRA, all the qualified distributions are tax-free to the second generation too.

ROTH IRAs TO HELP GRANDCHILDREN

The Roth IRA can be very effective when combined with certain trusts. Together, they can reduce taxes and provide tax-free growth when transferring assets to grandchildren.

You may be fortunate to have children who are doing very well financially. If you were planning to give them some of your assets they might say, "It's very nice of you to think of us, but we're doing ok and we're already paying very high taxes. Why don't you give them to the grandkids?"

When you plan to gift to grandchildren, you should be aware that there is a heavy Generation Skipping Transfer Tax (GSTT) imposed on large gifts of this type.

The latest Generation Skipping Transfer Tax was created in 1986 to thwart grandparents' attempts to pass large assets to grandchildren, great grandchildren and great great grandchildren without having it taxed at the death of the parents. Consequently, the IRS created rules that apply to assets going to "skip persons" who are family members two or more generations younger than the person giving the money, or non-family members at least 37.5 years younger.

There are certain types of gifts that are not subject to Generation Skipping Transfer Tax. These include any gifts that you make using the annual exemption from gift tax, which is $14,000 per donee in 2013. Also, if you pay medical expenses directly to a care provider or tuition payments directly to an educational institution for a grandchild, these would be tax-free gifts not subject to Generation Skipping Transfer Tax.

People make some common mistakes that cause them to pay more Generation Skipping Transfer Tax than they should. One of them is to not take advantage of the $5.25 million exemption. If you want certain assets to benefit grandchildren, make sure that the IRS knows about your intention to use some of your GSTT exemption. The best time to do this is on a gift-tax return filed the year after you make the transfer.

Another mistake is to wait until you die to use your GSTT exemption. Let's say that you have $100,000 that you want to set aside for the use of your grandchildren. This would be well within the GSTT exemption. You could put the money into an appropriate trust this year, inform the IRS that you exercised your GSTT exemption, and let it grow for their future use. By the time you pass away, it could have doubled or tripled but it would still be 100% GSTT free because the growth doesn't count. Therefore, it makes financial sense to use your GSTT exemption early, and apply it to assets that appreciate greatly in value or have a lot of leverage.

It used to be that when you passed assets to your grandchildren they could be taxed twice – once when they went to your children, and one more time when the children transferred them to the grandchildren.

The Generation-Skipping Trust avoids this double taxation and allows transfers directly to grandchildren with just one round of taxes. However, the IRS often gives with one hand and takes away with the other. This is also true of the Generation-Skipping Trust. As we mentioned earlier, taxable assets within the trust face the very highest marginal tax bracket (currently 39.6%).

This is where the Roth IRA comes into play. Even though assets in the Generation-Skipping Trust are subject to the maximum tax, the Roth IRA is by nature tax-free. Therefore, when you gift a Roth IRA into a Generation-Skipping Trust you get the all the tax benefits of generation-skipping but can also give your grandchildren tax-free growth.

THE 529 COLLEGE SAVINGS PLAN AS A MULTIGENERATIONAL PLANNING TOOL

It may seem odd to think of a college funding vehicle as a multigenerational planning tool, but the 529 College Savings Plan (named after a section of Internal Revenue Code) has emerged as just that.

To give a little history, the 529 plans came about as part of the Small Business Job Protection Act in 1996. Money contributed to a 529 plan can grow tax-deferred. And if the money is used for college tuition, room and board, equipment or books, the distributions can be federal income tax free. The money can be used at any accredited institution of higher learning within the U.S.

Contributions to 529 plans do not affect your child's or grandchild's eligibility for financial aid under the Federal Application For Student Aid, called FAFSA. This is because assets in the 529 plan are considered the property of the account owner who is generally the parent or grandparent. If the child owned the asset in his or her name, FAFSA would count 35% in its formula, potentially reducing eligibility for financial aid.

There are many grandparents who have IRAs and other retirement accounts. If they already have sufficient income through pensions, investments and rentals, they might not need to touch their retirement accounts. However, if they are age 70 ½ or older, they must take annual Required Minimum Distributions because the IRS mandates them.

They could put the Required Minimum Distributions into taxable accounts where dividends, interest and capital gains are taxed every year, or they could put it instead into 529 plans where the investments will grow tax-deferred, and can be distributed federal tax free to their beneficiaries. The difference in compounding between taxable accounts and tax-deferred accounts is significant over time.

In addition, those who want to gift money into a 529 plan can accelerate the gift. Normally, gifts are limited to $14,000 per year per recipient if you want to avoid gift tax. However, the 529 plan has special allowances that permit you to compress five years of gifting into the first year, gift up to $70,000 per recipient, and still avoid gift tax.

This means that parents or grandparents can gift up to $140,000 ($70,000 from the father and $70,000 from the mother) to each child in a lump sum without gift tax. The money would be outside of the donors' estate helping to reduce their liability for estate tax.

Beyond the financial advantages, a good education is one of the greatest gifts you can give to your grandchildren. A degree can open the door to good jobs, help establish their careers and move them towards independence and lifelong success. A gift doesn't get much better than that.

HOW TO USE LIFE INSURANCE IN MULTIGENERATIONAL PLANNING

One of our clients was concerned because he was planning to give his home to his daughter after he and his wife passed away. It was an expensive home in an affluent neighborhood, and he worried that his daughter would not be able to afford the property taxes, upkeep, and other expenses associated with the house and would eventually have to sell it.

He and his wife purchased what is called a "Second-To-Die" life insurance policy that would be payable income tax-free to their daughter after they both passed away. The death benefit from the policy could be invested in a diversified account and the growth of the investments could pay for ongoing expenses on the house indefinitely.

Because the Second-To-Die policy is a single policy that covers both the mother and father and pays off only after the second spouse passes away, it is more cost-effective than a policy covering only one person. The parents made their daughter the owner of the policy and they themselves were the insured persons. Structuring the policy this way made sure that the death benefit would go directly to their daughter rather than enlarging their own estate.

Each year when it came time to pay the premium on the insurance policy, the parents would gift the money to their daughter, their daughter would deposit the check into her account, and then write a personal check to the insurance company. This created a paper trail demonstrating to the IRS that the daughter was the bona fide owner of the policy.

BUSINESS STRUCTURES & MULTIGENERATIONAL PLANNING

If you own a family business or significant real estate holdings that you want to pass on to future generations, the type of business structure that you use can make a difference in the transfer.

There are various business structures available to you. Each has its pros and cons and suitability for different goals and types of companies. You should consult with a business attorney or CPA to discuss what structure might be best for you.

One of the most popular business structures is the Family Limited Partnership. In California, attorneys prefer a similar structure called the Limited Liability Company.

The right entity can give you the following benefits:
- Leverage the gifts
- Maintain control while holding a small percentage of ownership
- Protect the assets from creditors
- Protect the heirs from divorced spouses

One business owner, famous for effectively using the Family Limited Partnership, opened his retail store in Bentonville, Arkansas in the 1950s. It was called Walton's. When Sam Walton passed away in 1992 Wal-Mart was worth $25 billion. Thanks to his shrewd use of the Family Limited Partnership he was able to gift away 90% of the company to other family members before his death. This helped to reduce Sam Walton's estate tax liability. With the remaining 10% of the company he was able to maintain full control of Wal-Mart to the end.

This is because the Family Limited Partnership has both limited partners and general partners. Sam, as the general partner, made all the business decisions even though he held a small percentage of ownership. The limited partners owned most of the business for tax purposes but had little say-so in the day-to-day affairs of the company.

Being a general partner is like being the driver of a bus. The general partner occupies a small part of the bus but it's a critical part. The bus driver determines where the bus goes, when it stops, where it turns, who gets on and who gets off.

The limited partners are the passengers on the bus. They fill most of the bus but they have no control. However, they benefit by getting to their destination.

In the Family Limited Partnership the general partner calls the shots too – who's in, who's out, when distributions are made, the direction of the company and how the money is managed.

The limited partners pay taxes based on their pro-rata ownership of the company. Typically, the limited partners are in a lower tax bracket than the general partner, so this shifting of the tax burden makes financial sense.

It makes even more sense when the shifting of assets from the general partner to the limited partners receives a discount from the IRS. The creation of an FLP provides the opportunity for parents to gift more to their children and grandchildren than they could under ordinary circumstances. The amount that each person may gift to any one person each year without triggering Gift Tax is restricted by annual limits ($14,000 per person in 2013).

With an FLP, you can gift even more. This is because assets transferred within an FLP get a discount, often about 25%. The discount is based on the fact that the value of the pieces is less than the whole. The children receiving shares within the FLP have no management control of the assets, and the shares are not marketable. Obviously, a non-controlling interest has less value, and the IRS accepts this. In this way, parents can gift more in actual value than the annual gifting limits would normally allow.

These discounts are valuable, especially when the assets are growing rapidly within the Family Limited Partnership or Limited Liability Company and you are running out of time. If the shares of the FLP were discounted by 25% you could gift $18,666 worth of shares per year and still be counted for only $14,000.

The other important advantage of the FLP is the ability to freeze the value of the assets. After shares are gifted to the limited partners they are likely to grow in value. However, in the eyes of the IRS they retain their original value. In other words, the growth isn't counted.

The FLP serves the valuable function of keeping assets in the family. Ownership of partnership interests typically is limited to members of the same family unit. This has enabled many FLPs to stay within the family for several generations.

Many parents are concerned about what will happen to family assets in the event their children get divorced. The protection provided by the FLP works well under these circumstances. The parents can transfer the child's limited partner interest to a trust to be held for the child's lifetime. The child benefits from full use and control of the assets during his or her lifetime, but technically does not own the asset. If there is a divorce, the asset is protected from the ex-spouse.

The Family Limited Partnership may offer wealth transfer opportunities and protection for your family that are not possible with other strategies. You should consult your Certified Financial Planner™, tax and legal advisors to determine if the FLP or LLC would be appropriate for your particular situation. It can provide a valuable added dimension that is easily integrated with your existing multigenerational plan.

LONG INVESTMENT HORIZON STRATEGIES

Multigenerational planning opens up doors to investment strategies that were unavailable to previous generations except for the very wealthy. They have to do with having a longer investment horizon than most people are accustomed to thinking about. It's a different mindset.

We used to wonder why some corporations and institutions were able to get extraordinary returns on their investments. One big reason is that they have a longer investment horizon than other investors. Most of us think only in terms of our own life expectancy. We gravitate towards the kind of investments that will give a good return while we're still living.

Corporations and institutions think differently because they have the advantage of time. They can wait longer than an average life expectancy for an investment to grow and mature. An institution like USC can buy up property in downtown Los Angeles when it's dirt cheap, wait 50 to 75 years for the downtown area to become gentrified, and then sell it at a huge profit.

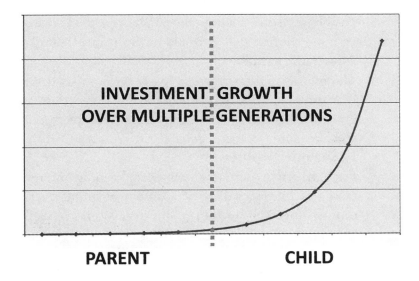

If you could expand your investment horizon to include that of your children and grandchildren, you could also take advantage of these long-term strategies. There are tried-and-true methods that the wealthiest families have used for generations to allow this to happen. These strategies are available to everyone.

One of most effective of these is the Dynasty Trust.

THE DYNASTY TRUST

The Dynasty Trust allows you to trade Ownership for Control. The government tends to tax what people own, not what they control. People sue each other for what they own, and not very successfully for what they control. So in a perfect world, you would own nothing and control everything.

We currently have a set of circumstances that make the Dynasty Trust even more effective than it would normally be. They are:

- **Affordable values**

    The market is on a tear but many economists think that stocks are not overpriced and still have room to grow. Real estate is recovering quickly but prices are still affordable in many areas of the country.

- **Lower interest rates**

    Fed Chairman Bernanke has been keeping interest rates low by purchasing $85 billion of bonds every month since the bottom of the recession. He can't keep it up much longer without risking inflation, and the improving economy makes it difficult for him to continue. His talk of "tapering back" on bond purchases has already put interest rates on the upswing. Still, in historical terms interest rates are still low.

Affordable values and low interest rates mean that assets that you put into a Dynasty Trust now have a good chance of appreciating in value over the next few years. You can watch those assets rebound in value inside the Dynasty Trust exempt from estate taxes.

Here's how the Dynasty Trust works. First, you transfer assets to their Dynasty Trust. You can use any type of asset that grows well. Once the assets are inside the Dynasty Trust they have the following protections and benefits:

- The assets inside the Dynasty Trust avoid estate taxes
- The assets are protected against the claims of creditors and ex-spouses
- Funds inside the Dynasty Trust can be used to provide education funding, business start-up funds and financial security for generations to come.

- Many families use the Dynasty Trust as a "family bank" to provide low-interest or no-interest loans to family members.

ADJUSTING INVESTMENT STRATEGIES FOR MULTIGENERATIONAL GOALS

Investing for multiple generations can require a different approach compared to investing just for yourself. The good news is that it involves getting a better return with less risk.

We mentioned in the chapter on "Investing for Retirement" that there are two main risks when it comes to investing. One is Purchasing Power Risk and the other is Principal Risk. They behave very differently from one another, opposites in fact.

Purchasing Power Risk is driven by inflation. It's relentless like waves against rocks and just as powerful. Unless your nest egg is invested to keep pace with inflation and hopefully exceed it, the money can decline over time and eventually run out.

Principal Risk is the risk of losing your capital. It behaves just the opposite of Purchasing Power Risk – it declines over time and eventually goes to zero. Time is its friend.

What that means for the multigenerational investor is that he or she can take advantage of time, invest for a little more growth and do it at relatively low Principal Risk. The added growth that you receive helps to defeat Purchasing Power Risk. Your assets then have the potential to grow for generations, having a broad, ripple effect.

Choose a financial advisory firm that can help you maintain continuity in your multigenerational investment strategy. Your advisory firm may have to begin the strategy in one generation and complete it in the next. A sole practitioner financial advisor may not have the longevity to complete this type of plan. The frequent turn-over among bank financial advisors makes them less than ideal as well. You should look for a firm that has a stable history, has a long-term commitment to their clients, and has an internal succession plan designed to provide ongoing multigenerational care and advice.

You will also want to introduce your children or other beneficiaries to your Certified Financial Planner™. They don't need to know all the details of your plan right now unless you want to share them. However, it will be important for them to know your objectives and the advisor that they can turn to if anything happens to you.

FAMILY UNITY & MULTIGENERATIONAL PLANNING

Too many brothers and sisters have not talked to each other for the rest of their lives after their parents passed away because of the conflict created by poor planning or lack of planning.

A couple of years ago, AARP [Washington Post, EP file, 1] released a study that found that one in five people receiving an inheritance battled over it with other family members. The worst combatants were Baby Boomers age 50 to 63, with a third of them reporting squabbles. It doesn't have to be that way if the parents follow a few sensible ideas.

When it comes to the question of how much to give to each child, parents often ask, "Should I be equal, or should I be fair?" In other words, should you give an equal amount to each child regardless of their circumstances and earning potential, or make a judgment about how much to give each child based on his or her need for assets and income. Although it's not a hard and fast rule, many families find that it's better to be equal. Each child will make life choices for him or herself, has to live by those choices and will learn through making those choices. The parents ultimately won't help this learning process if they always intervene to make everything right.

Whether a child is rich or poor, he or she often sees the inheritance as a measure of the parents' love. If one child receives more than another, it can be a source of friction and incriminations long after the parents have died.

Another common question is, "How much is enough, and how much is too much?" Someone asked Warren Buffett the same question and he replied, "I want my children to have enough money that they can do anything, but not so much that they can do nothing."

Studies of affluent families have shown that heirs who receive too much wealth often feel low self-esteem and lack of personal independence. Rather than feeling that they are blessed with advantages they often suffer from isolation and alienation, a feeling that life is passing them by.

You may have heard stories of children who quit their jobs because they expected a substantial inheritance from their parents, or about people who lived alienated, troubled lives because of inherited wealth. Whether you are affluent or not, you have to consider the fine line between providing enough for your heirs and providing too much.

Heirs who are unprepared for an inheritance can experience a sense of guilt because they didn't "earn" the money. Or they may live a life filled with anxiety and stress because they are worried that they may lose it all by becoming victims of fraud and con artists.

Your own success in life may have been motivated by doing without (or at least not having everything you wanted) earlier in life. It may have forced you to create a plan for your future, discipline yourself to carry out that plan, persist through obstacles and setbacks, and finally enjoy the fruits of your hard work.

Japanese Americans have worked hard, demonstrated creativity, and made a mark even in the face of severe hardship and discrimination. You might hope, as we do, that your children and grandchildren can build upon what you already accomplished and achieve even loftier goals. You may also want them to have a safety net, so if they trip and fall, they won't suffer irreparable harm. In your effort to protect your family and provide financial security you may run the risk of causing just the opposite effect.

How can you pass on your assets in a "good" way? First of all, you want to look out for yourself and have enough income so you will be comfortable for the rest of your life and be able to do all the things you want to do, with room to spare. You also want to have some assets in reserve to take care of any emergencies. You will have to determine for yourself, with help from your Certified Financial Planner™, what the actual numbers will be.

Once you subtract those numbers from your total income and assets, you will know how much you can allocate to other people, including your children. In the same way that you did for yourself, you and your financial planner estimate what income and assets your children will need for their health, education, maintenance and support. Subtract from this amount what you expect your children to earn and contribute on their own.

Some parents write their trusts in such a way that the children must meet certain conditions before they can access any trust assets. For example, if a child earns money on his own, the trust can pay out a matching amount for each dollar earned. If the child earns no income there would be no payment from the trust.

You may worry about a child that has a drug or drinking problem, or is not good at managing money. The way a living trust is written can also overcome some of these concerns. For example, the trust could pay a larger amount or pay it sooner if the child graduates from college, maintains a certain grade point average, or stays free of drugs, alcohol or tobacco.

The key is to discuss these restrictions with your children beforehand. This not only helps minimize misunderstandings, but also helps your children plan their own financial life. Simply cutting a child out of a will can provoke ill feelings not only toward you, but also create a lifelong resentment toward those children who did inherit.

PLANNING FOR SPECIAL NEEDS

If one of your children is disabled and has special needs, it requires special planning and thought. As a parent, you want to make sure this child is cared for even when you're no longer around. However, a dilemma occurs because if you give assets directly to this child, your gift can disqualify him or her from important government benefits and support. This is especially true of Medicaid (called Medi-Cal in California) since it's a needs-based program. Medicaid can provide medical care for your disabled child for a lifetime. It is a safety net you don't want to jeopardize.

The solution is to create a Special Needs Trust for the child. The assets you place in the trust are there for all the things that government programs don't pay for. However, the disabled child does not control the assets in the trust. It is managed by a trustee, who can be yourself while you're living and one of your other children as successor trustee when you pass away. Because your disabled child does not "own" the assets, he or she is still eligible for public programs.

SHOULD I SHARE MY PLAN WITH MY CHILDREN?

Discussing your multigenerational plan in advance with your children can improve the probability of success. Introducing them to a trusted financial professional while you are still living can also give them greater confidence to move forward.

Some parents involve their adult children in their planning and others prefer to keep the matter to themselves. It's a personal decision. However there is one decision in which you should have your children's input. Who should be the executor of the estate after both parents pass away? You probably want it to be one or more of the children and have a pretty good idea who it should be, but your children may have different ideas. You don't want your children to have to thrash this out after you're gone.

Involve your children in the discussion about who should take the responsibility of being executor. When the time comes to take the reins, your executor or co-executors will be prepared for the task and have the support of the other siblings.

This can also be a good time to talk about who gets or wants certain heirlooms or memorabilia. Some of the biggest battles among heirs are over personal items that sometimes have little monetary value. Write these decisions out in a letter of instruction that accompanies your will, explaining who should receive particular items.

We have found that Japanese Americans generally don't feel comfortable with over-complexity in their estate planning. Nor do they tend to favor strategies that are too aggressive and on the "bleeding edge" of planning theory. What is tried and true, unassuming and simple fits the bill.

Therefore, if a financial planner presents you with two proposals that provide similar results, but one is complex and the other is relatively simple, we suggest that you take the simpler choice. You will probably be happier in the long run and have more peace of mind not worrying about the administration of your plan or possible IRS challenges.

The point of multigenerational planning is to provide future security for your family and create the conditions where your children can remain good friends after you're gone. The good example that you set for your children can be the final parental legacy that you leave to them.

CREATING A MULTIGENERATIONAL PLAN

The initial step in applying these multigenerational strategies for your family is to create a plan that is tailored to your needs.

A house starts with a blueprint. Your multigenerational plan also has a blueprint, called a Multigeneration Plan Design. Your Certified Financial Planner™ can be the quarterback for creating this design with input from your CPA and attorney.

The process is similar to bringing together the architect, electricians, plumbers, stone masons and other builders to construct your dream home.

The plan your advisors collectively bring to you represents their best ideas from a financial, legal and tax point of view (see the chapter on "The Collaborative Process").

Once you approve the Multigeneration Plan Design, your advisors get to work implementing it. When electricians, plumbers and stone masons all work from the same blueprint, the integrity of your home tends to reflect it. Your Multigeneration Plan's high probability of success also demonstrates the depth of thought and coordination that went into it.

Multigenerational planning is done most effectively as a co-ordinated strategy with input from all family members. It makes it possible for subsequent generations to build upon the accomplishments of their parents and grandparents and reach new heights.

CHAPTER 13

JAPANESE AMERICANS
& GIVING

M any Japanese Americans have very strong ties to their community churches, temples and organizations. This was cemented many generations ago when their ancestors first came to the U.S., often with just a few dollars in their pockets. Frequently they were teenagers who came alone with no family and they knew no one when they stepped off the boat. They might not have survived without the help of a "kenjinkai" (provincial club) or "tanomoshi" (fraternal organization).

They depended on the generosity and network of these organizations for moral support, introductions to employers and services, and financial help when times were tough. In the face of anti-Asian legislation and lynch mobs, the organizations also provided physical protection and legal advice.

It is no surprise that community groups continue to be held in high esteem, and preservation of the Japanese American community remains a priority for many individuals and families. However, the Great Recession took a heavy toll on these groups and many of them are still struggling for survival.

THE TRADITION OF GIVING

Japanese Americans who have made a mark, achieved great things and excelled in their life's work know they didn't do it alone. Other people nurtured them, mentored them, gave them advice, introduced them to the right people, and recommended them to their friends. Many successful Japanese Americans feel that they want to give something back to the community, to a church, temple, school, community organization or museum. They want to leave something behind to help others, in the same way that other people helped them.

George Aratani, founder of Mikasa and Kenwood, created the Aratani Foundation in 1994, providing support to more than 140 community organizations. He was awarded the "Kunsho," Order of the Sacred Treasure, Gold Rays

 *with Rosette, from the Japanese government.*

Sakaye Aratani was the first Nisei woman to be awarded a "Kunsho," Fourth-Class Order of the Sacred Treasure, for her service to numerous community organizations includ-ing the Montebello Japanese Women's Club, City View Hospital, Keiro Senior HealthCare and the Japanese American Cultural and Community Center.

Today, new community organizations and institutions help Japanese Americans preserve their history, engage in athletic competition such as youth basketball leagues, have a voice in the arts and media, gain affordable housing, get legal help, and receive care when they can no longer care for themselves.

However, these organizations would quickly wither away without individual support. Corporate and foundation grants only account for a small proportion of the total funding for most charitable organizations. Nationally, small, individual donations account for about 90% of total support dollars.

DON'T FORGET YOUR SOCIAL LEGACY

We mentioned in the previous chapter on Multigenerational Planning that a good plan will provide enough income to the parents so they can do all the things on their "bucket list" and have assets in reserve to take care of any emergencies. The plan is also designed to provide financial security for their children and grandchildren that is "just right" without diminishing their motivation to excel in their own goals and careers and reach their greatest potential. You may still have assets left over that you can allocate to a broader and higher purpose.

If the only thing that you pass to your family is your financial wealth, you may be doing a disservice to yourself and your heirs. Your social legacy is at least as important as your financial legacy. Your involvement in philanthropy, and the involvement of your family, provides a way to pass on your personal values and sense of community responsibility. You may be dead and gone, but your children, your grandchildren and your great grandchildren can be more rounded and productive people because of your leadership and example.

PARTNERING WITH YOUR TEMPLE, CHURCH OR COMMUNITY ORGANIZATION

The IRS supports you in this effort and offers encouragement in the form of tax incentives that benefit not only the community organizations but your estate as well.

Usually, the IRS tends to penalize you for investing too wisely and being too smart. When you make a good investment and it appreciates in value you may find that the value is effectively locked up because the investment can't be sold without incurring capital gains tax. A very effective way to unlock these assets so you and your family can use them is to partner with a Not-For-Profit Organization or NPO.

You and your family may have owned income property for a long time. There are two benefits of owning real estate: one is the increase in value of the property, and the other is the tax benefit through depreciation. Your property may already be fully depreciated, which means you are no longer receiving any tax benefit. You then have the following choices:
- You can die with the property, in which case your children can get a step-up in basis. This means the capital gains are waived, and your heirs can then sell the property without the burden of capital gains tax.

However dying is not always an attractive option. You may prefer to spend and enjoy the assets while you're alive. Perhaps you would like to give something to your children now rather than later, or maybe you have no children or heirs.

- If you sell the property you must pay about 20% tax on the gain (approximately 15% Federal and 5% State). Often this tax is greater than what you paid originally for the property.
- You could do a 1031 exchange. Using this provision of the Internal Revenue Code, you can exchange your old property for new property. By doing so, you can benefit from depreciation all over again. However, you're continuing to manage property again. If you are in retirement you may no longer want to deal with fixing toilets, collecting rent and the challenges of finding good tenants.
- The fourth choice may be the most attractive -partnering with a Not-For-Profit Organization. The benefits can be impressive. You can sell highly appreciated assets such as stocks and real estate while avoiding the immediate hit from capital gains tax. You have the potential to increase your income compared to what you were earning in rental income or dividends. You can reduce your income tax for as long as six years through a tax deduction. Finally, you may pass assets to your children and grandchildren free of gift and estate tax.

How does this work? The same Internal Revenue Code that established gift and estate taxes also laid out the tools that allow you to minimize or even completely avoid the tax. In 1969, Congress passed IRC Section 664 which allowed a "charitable deduction for a contribution in trust of a remainder interest or an income interest in property." What this means in plain English is that through a device called a

Charitable Remainder Trust you can pass appreciated assets to a Not-For-Profit organization such as a museum, church, college, media arts organization, hospital or community center. These organizations are exempt from income taxes and capital gains taxes and so they may then sell the appreciated assets without paying capital gains taxes.

The NPO promises to pay the donor monthly or annual payments a term of years or for the rest of his or her life. This income stream is often greater than the income the donor was receiving from the original asset and greater than the net proceeds if he or she had sold the asset themselves.

The donor can also take an income tax deduction for the estimated value that will end up going to the charity. The claim is entered in the 1040 tax return, Schedule A, Itemized Deductions under a section called Gifts to Charity. In practice, what this means is that at least 10% of the value of the assets must end up going to the NPO. When you establish a Charitable Remainder Trust this tax deduction is often so large that you cannot use it all in one year. Fortunately, the IRS allows you to take the tax deduction in the year of the gift plus carry it forward for five additional years.

The advantages are similar for people who have stocks that have appreciated considerably in value. Suppose you bought a stock many years ago for $10 a share. Now after splitting several times it's worth $100 a share and may not be paying much in dividends. You may be reluctant to sell these because it would trigger too much capital gain tax. Again, the best solution may be to work together with a Non-Profit Organization.

The NPO could sell the stock and replace it with an income-producing asset without paying tax on the transaction. You would benefit from the increased income, and receive a charitable deduction as well. The charity would receive a very welcome donation that helps support its services. You would have helped to make the community a better place.

By use of these and other tools, it's possible to significantly reduce the tax burden of your estate. In some cases it is even possible to establish a zero tax estate plan. Judge Learned Hand, who served on the U.S. Court of Appeals back in the 1940s said, "There are two systems of taxation in this country, one for the informed and one for the uninformed."

By working with a NPO you have the opportunity to become one of the informed. The relationship could save you a bundle in income and estate taxes, give you increased income to spend during your lifetime, and contribute to the long-term financial health of your favorite community organization.

GIVING MADE SIMPLE

Using a charitable remainder trust is only one of many ways to participate in charitable giving. In fact, 70% of individual gifts to charitable organizations are through simple bequests in wills or living trusts. Other forms of giving include charitable lead trusts, charitable gift annuities and donations of used automobiles and other vehicles.

Charitable planning can be very simple. If you are 70 ½ or older, you can make a direct contribution of as much as $100,000 from your IRA to a non-profit organization. This can have some very beneficial tax consequences.

Normally, when you take a distribution from your IRA it is fully-taxable at ordinary income rates. After taxes are deducted, you have a net amount that you can spend or donate. When you make a direct transfer from your IRA to an NPO, there are no taxes due to you, and the charity receives full value with no taxes removed. Make sure that the custodian of the IRA drafts the check in the charity's name, not yours.

If you are younger than 70 ½, you can accomplish the same thing but in a two-step process. First you take a normal distribution from your IRA in your own name. You will receive a 1099 for the tax at the end of the year. However, when you donate the distribution to charity, you receive a tax deduction. The 1099 is cancelled out by the tax deduction and you should pay no taxes on the distribution.

Another uncomplicated strategy is to gift a life insurance policy to a charitable organization. This works best when the policy is a type that has cash value, like whole life or universal life. We have seen policies that clients purchased 30 years ago in order to pay off the mortgage balance on their home or self-complete college funding for their toddler children in case they died prematurely. Now their home is paid off and their children are grown and graduated but they still have the life insurance policy.

They could terminate the policy and receive the cash value but they may have to pay taxes on any gain in the policy. A better use might be to transfer ownership to their favorite community organization. The donors would receive a tax deduction for the cash value. The community organization would benefit in two ways —

- The charitable organization would receive the full cash value without any taxes due. They could borrow from the cash value to help fund current programs.
- It could continue to pay the premiums on the policy to keep it in force and receive the death benefit income tax-free when the policy holder passes away. This would help to create an endowment fund for the organization and build long-term financial stability.

PERSONAL LEGACY SUPPORTS FINANCIAL LEGACY

By keeping the community in mind when you plan, you are able to transfer not only your financial legacy but your personal legacy as well. Your personal legacy includes your values and the purpose of your life. Without the personal legacy to support it, the financial legacy could fall under its own weight. Financial assets are most valuable when they are in the hands of children and grandchildren who are confident in who they are, feel empowered and supported, and can use the monetary advantage to create true personal independence for themselves, greater happiness for their families, and benefit for their communities.

"Life has been good to Ruri and me. If we're in a position to return some of the good fortune that we've realized, we should do it. We want to give back, what the community has been able to give to us." – George Sugimoto

George Sugimoto founded KGS electronics in 1959, building the company into a leading designing and manufacturing firm in the aviation industry, worldwide.

Through the Sugimoto Family Foundation, George, Ruri and their children, Lisa and Nathan, have supported the Japanese American National Museum, the Japanese American Culture Community Center, Keiro Senior Healthcare, the East San Gabriel Valley Community Center, Neighbors Active Together Helping All, the Heads Up Youth Foundation, and Asia America Symphony Assoc. & Guild, among many others.

CHAPTER 14

THERE ARE FINANCIAL ADVISORS, & THEN THERE ARE FINANCIAL ADVISORS

THE BROKER MODEL VS. THE FIDUCIARY MODEL

"Financial advisors" come in all shapes and sizes. There are over a hundred designations for financial advisors, ranging for those that require years of study and multiple difficult examinations to those that require a half-day online course with a quiz at the end. Some designations are awarded for meeting certain sales targets, rather than for knowledge or competence. This can be a source of confusion.

Japanese Americans generally don't have a long history in their families of working with financial professionals. One reason is that past experiences with financial institutions have not always been good. During World War II, while they were imprisoned in U.S. concentration camps, the American Superintendent of Banks froze Japanese American bank accounts. Although they were cut off from their funds they were still held liable for non-payment of mortgages, insurance premiums, property taxes and other bills. Many families lost what little they had through foreclosure and confiscation. It's no wonder that many Japanese Americans still associate financial institutions, attorneys and the justice system with economic devastation and view them with suspicion.

Many of our clients are incredibly nice people. This has sometimes caused them to be victimized in the past by a pushy "financial advisor." They bought an investment or insurance product they really didn't like because they didn't want to hurt the agent's feelings. More than once, people have described how an agent wouldn't take "No" for an answer and refused to leave their home until they signed on the dotted line. The intimidation and pressure unleashed on these families made them resolve to never face another financial advisor again.

Many Japanese Americans have gone to the bank to review their Certificates of Deposit, and have been steered towards the bank's "financial advisor." The family hopes that their bank, where they entrust their savings, will do the right thing for them. They hope that the professional-looking person who appears before them must know what he or she is talking about and is working in the family's best interest. A common outcome of this meeting is the purchase of an annuity whether or not it meets the family's financial needs and goals. The family does not realize that much of the bank's and the "financial advisor's" income is derived from selling certain annuities and that they are primarily looking out for their own bottom line.

If this is similar to your own experience with the financial services industry, you have a lot to overcome. Your financial future is too important to be sidetracked by historical injustices or past, questionable sales practices.

It may be helpful to know that the hundreds of "financial advisor" designations fall into two important categories: brokers and fiduciaries. Brokers are sales people. Fiduciaries are advisors who are required to place the interests of their clients first.

Brokers are allowed to sell the products that are most profitable for them, even if they may not be the ones that best meet their clients' needs and goals. The guideline for brokers is "suitability." As long as a product is "suitable" for a client, then the broker is free to choose the one that is most profitable to him or her.

Fiduciaries must meet a higher standard. They are obligated to give their clients objective advice and always act in their best interests. They must thoroughly disclose to their clients information about the services they provide, the fees or commissions they receive and any conflicts of interest in the recommendations that they make. If they fail to do so, they could lose their licenses. Your attorney and CPA are fiduciaries. So are Certified Financial Planners™ and Registered Investment Advisors.

Certified Financial Planners™ and Registered Investment Advisors know that the only values that keep them in business are their integrity and their service. If they put their own interests before their clients' or treat their clients in an unethical manner, word gets around very quickly. This is especially true in the Japanese American community where it sometimes feels like everyone knows everyone. There are many reputable financial professionals in your community. Ask your friends for a recommendation.

Look for a Certified Financial Planner™ who does it full-time. In order to do a good job, a financial planner must keep up not only with his clients' changing life circumstances, but also with fluctuating markets, new products and strategies, and evolving tax legislation. To do this requires hours of annual Continuing Education study, attendance at industry conferences and workshops, and sharing best practices with other financial professionals. It will be very difficult for a planner who is holding down two jobs to maintain competency in both areas.

Sometimes a "financial advisor" will attempt to sell you a product before he or she knows much about you and your family's values, goals, financial circumstances and needs. This approach is a giveaway, and marks a sales-oriented company culture. It is characterized by a carefully scripted discussion that leads you towards a purchase, and optional scripts to overcome objections should you balk. It will be quickly evident to you that the consultant is more intent on his goal, which is to close the sale, rather than yours. You should feel no embarrassment about ending the meeting and leaving. A good Certified Financial Planner™, similar to a good physician, will complete a thorough examination, conduct a careful analysis, and make a diagnosis before writing a prescription.

You should look for a financial advisor who has a certification that requires him to be a fiduciary.

Some nationally recognized fiduciary certifications are Certified Financial Planner™ (CFP), granted by the Certified Financial Planner Board of Standards; Chartered Financial Consultant (ChFC), awarded by the American College; Personal Financial Specialist (PFS), accredited by the American Institute of CPAs, and Certified Financial Analyst (CFA) awarded by the CFA Institute Board of Governors. These people have invested the time to study and have passed difficult exams in order to meet the standards of the industry. In order to keep their accreditation, they must satisfy ongoing Continuing Education and Ethics requirements. Although finding an advisor with a certification is not a guarantee of integrity or knowledge, it's a better bet than working with someone who has not made the effort.

Your decision to work with a financial planner should be undertaken with the same care that you would use to select a physician, dentist, accountant or attorney.

How Financial Advisors Are Compensated

Investing is complex, and most people already have full-time jobs, or if they are retired, have better ways to spend their time. Studying optimization tables or comparing efficient frontiers and standard deviations pales against traveling to Paris or taking the grandkids on a Disney cruise.

How does the average investor implement an investment strategy that meets their particular family goals? For most people, the most efficient way is to hire an investment professional. However, there are wide differences in methodology and approach.

Some advisors don't pay much attention to asset allocation or diversification. Their approach is to sell you the latest hot fund or stock. They may present you with detailed charts and graphs, but they can only tell you how a stock or fund has performed in the past not how it will fare in the future.

Others will use asset allocation (a method for diversifying your investments), and fill the slots with funds and individual securities that they researched themselves or that were recommended by their broker dealer's research service. The problem here is that their broker dealer often has its own agenda and "encourages" their reps to promote certain investments, which may or may not be the very best choices for your particular goals.

We believe a better approach is to use asset allocation and implement it with objective money management specialists. The money managers often employ a worldwide research staff of Chartered Financial Analysts and PhDs in order to do effective analysis and to keep up with today's global markets. It's what they do best. The advisor, then, focuses on what he does best which is to serve his clients and help them achieve their goals and priorities.

Some advisors get paid by commission-only, usually 5 to 6% on mutual fund transactions and as high as 15% on some annuities. Long ago, this was the primary method of compensation.

Others advisors get paid by fee-only, and charge you to create a financial plan, and then an annual fee of 1 to 2% of your assets under management.

Many advisors fall somewhere in the middle, called "fee-based." These advisors take fees rather than commissions on investments to reduce costs to clients. For products that have not yet developed a fee structure, like life insurance and long term care insurance, they will take commission and always disclose to clients exactly how they are being compensated.

When an advisor is commission-only, he depends on the client making a transaction in order to make money. Many people who work with this type of advisor complain that the only time they get a call from the advisor is when he wants them to buy something. It puts clients in the awkward position of always having to second-guess the stockbroker. Is he encouraging this transaction because it's good for the client or because it's good for him?

The other problem with commissioned stockbrokers is service. Once he has made his commission, there's little incentive for him to provide ongoing service. He's already received everything he's going to get, up front. The common complaint here is that after the initial sale, the client often never sees the advisor again.

When an advisor is fee-only or fee-based, there is no incentive to make unnecessary, short-term trades to generate commissions. Instead, he or she wants to build a long-term relationship with the client. Because the advisor depends on receiving smaller, annual fees, he or she is motivated to keep the client happy through better reporting, ongoing good service and prompt communication. It is a requirement for these advisors to meet their clients on a regular basis to review the plan, make adjustments for changing personal circumstances, market conditions and tax laws, and keep them on track towards their goals.

One of the most important roles of an advisor is to help clients through periods of economic uncertainty and stick to the plan that they created together. The longer you hold an investment, the better your chances are for a significant gain. However, the tendency is great for individual investors to get discouraged by short-term results or rattled by media hype. The first three years of an investment are the hardest to get through because this is when the fluctuation is greatest. A good advisor helps his clients fight fear and make it through the rough spots.

YOUR INITIAL APPOINTMENT

The financial planning process is designed to create more peace of mind now, better confidence in the future, and a greater probability of attaining important goals. People working with financial advisors tend to be better at accomplishing their goals than those who don't. Perhaps it's because working with a financial professional helps them to stick to their plan. The first step in the process is an initial consultation with a Certified Financial Planner™.

The initial meeting is often free. This is because CFPs don't know until they meet you whether they can actually help you or not. Although they all took similar courses and examinations, their practices are individually designed to serve the clients they can benefit most. Some CFPs are jacks-of-all-trades, many CFPs specialize in investment management only, and most are somewhere in the middle.

By the end of the meeting, the planner should be able to tell you what he or she can do for you and how much it may cost. You will probably be given options ranging from a Comprehensive Financial Plan to a single product or service.

If what you really need is an attorney or a CPA, the advisor will tell you so.

One of the most common and fundamental questions a new client will ask a financial planner is, "How much do I need to save for retirement – just a ballpark figure." The planner might smile because this is also one of the most difficult questions to answer. Here's why.

Calculating how much you need for retirement is different for each person and is both a science and an art. Everyone's goals, lifestyles and circumstances are unique. To answer the question accurately requires not only an in-depth discussion with the client about hopes and dreams, but also the use of sophisticated software (the science) and the planner's experience with other clients (the art) to evaluate the impact of each of the following factors: life expectancy, desired investment return, risk tolerance, average annual expenses, anticipated medical needs, responsibilities to parents and children, the economic and market environment, inflation, and much more. There are whole books written to describe the process and how to implement it. It would be a disservice to try to present it in full here, and your financial advisor will tailor the process to your individual needs anyway.

The preparation and thought that you bring to your initial meeting with your Certified Financial Planner™ can make all the difference in creating the most accurate and useful plan. Following is a list of the items that you should bring to your initial meeting so your planner can begin determining your retirement needs:
- Most recent tax returns
- Copy of your will and trust

- Most recent investment/brokerage statement
- Retirement plan statements from work – i.e.: 401(k), 403(b), 457, SEP IRA, Simple IRA
- Liquid accounts – i.e.: CDs, credit union accounts, savings, money market
- Most recent annuity statements and the original annuity policies
- Copies of your life insurance policies
- Real estate investments or limited partnership investments with original cost and approximate current value
- Social Security benefits statement – for future or current income benefits
- Pension income sources, payout structure and benefit amount
- Your best estimate of your current annual living expenses and anticipated costs in retirement. This should include health costs, meals and entertainment, travel expenses, mortgage, etc.)

CFPs™ know the preparation takes some work. They also recognize how much commitment it took on the part of their clients to come to the initial meeting. Good advisors take their responsibility seriously and reciprocate clients' trust by becoming a true partner in their future.

CHAPTER 15

THE COLLABORATIVE PROCESS

HOW YOUR PROFESSIONAL ADVISORS WORK AS A TEAM TO ACCOMPLISH YOUR GOALS

With today's ever-changing tax laws and challenging economic conditions, we feel it is crucial for professional advisors like Attorneys, CPAs and Certified Financial Planners™ to continually invest in ways that will enhance the financial stability and security of their clients. Their ability to work well with each other is an important part of this process.

In order to facilitate team-building among our clients' advisors, we joined WealthCounsel several years ago. It is a national group of like-minded Attorney's, CPAs and Certified Financial Planners™ who have come together to better serve their clients. It has earned great respect as one of the foremost proponents of collaboration among professional advisors. We believe this approach represents the new model for effective financial planning and estate planning. It leads to better service and improved strategies for our clients.

THE OLD PROCESS

In the past, one of the greatest obstacles in financial planning and estate planning was the inability of the client's professional advisors to find a common ground. Some Attorneys and CPAs perceived Certified Financial Planners to be merely product pushers and disdained their suggestions if they were unfamiliar. Some Certified Financial Planners viewed CPAs and Attorneys as obstacles when they told the client not to move forward with the advisor's recommendations. Attorneys resented being relegated to the role of scrivener, simply drafting documents without any input in the process. All suffered to some degree from the Not-Invented-Here syndrome. In other words if they did not come up with the strategy themselves they would sometimes reject an otherwise appropriate recommendation.

The outcome was that the client would receive different and often conflicting recommendations from the CPA, Attorney and Certified Financial Planner. Typically this would end in confusion and lack of confidence. The financial plan or estate plan, even if it was brilliant, did not advance the client's financial security and stability because it sat on his or her shelf and was never implemented.

THE COLLABORATIVE PROCESS

In the collaborative process the Attorney, CPA and Certified Financial Planner are all involved in the strategy development process. Together they evaluate the best possible strategies and narrow them down to those that are most valuable in accomplishing the client's goals. The synergistic process takes full advantage of each professional advisor's core expertise. It tends to result in a better, more thought-out plan.

When clients receive plan designs that have the collective endorsement and best thinking of all of their professional advisors, they have a higher regard for all of them and are much more confident to move forward and carry out their recommendations. Best of all, clients are then free to focus on their most important goals – their families and communities.

THE COLLABORATIVE PRINCIPLES

The collaborative process is based on five important principles:
- A commitment to the success of the clients.
- Understanding and respecting the knowledge, experience and perspectives of all of the professional advisors.
- Creating a venue for consistent networking, relationship-building and sharing of knowledge.
- Staying up-to-date with changing tax laws and new strategies that may benefit the client.
- Demonstrating a willingness to work with other professional advisors to provide client-centered services.

We hope that by extending ourselves to other professional advisors and participating in WealthCounsel's continuing education program we will all be more effective in helping our clients build, maintain and transfer their wealth.

CHAPTER 16

NOW WHAT?

MONEY IS JUST WHAT GETS YOU THERE

Many financial planners agree that just helping their clients make smart financial decisions is not enough. It's very possible to have more assets and income than you need and still have an unhappy and unfulfilling retirement. The emphasis in financial planning is moving towards helping clients achieve their life goals and ensuring that they achieve a quality of life that is emotionally rewarding.

You've heard the term, "You can't take it with you." In a world where we have more things to buy and more toys to play with than ever before, the adage still holds true. You've probably laughed at the other common saying, "The one who dies with the most toys wins," because you knew in your heart that it wasn't true.

The things that make you truly a "winner" in life are usually not material at all. They have more to do with love of friends and family, good health, a positive relationship with your spouse, fulfillment in your career, spiritual peace, involvement in your community, and other goals that are not financial in nature.

Money plays a supportive role, and is the means rather than the end. If life were like a road trip, money is like the gasoline you put in your car. It's the fuel that moves you along life's highway and gets you to your destination.

PLAN YOUR RETIREMENT "OCCUPATION"

Many people who have had meaningful careers find their personal identity is wrapped up in their work. When we were working and people asked us what we did we could reply, "I'm a business owner," or, "I'm an attorney," or, "I'm a teacher." When we retire we lose that identity. People start asking, "Weren't you Dr. Sato?" We may respond, "I'm retired now," but that doesn't have quite the same ring.

The most successful retirees are those who plan their future lives well before they get to age 65. They don't want to re-tire *from* something – they want something to retire *to*. The earlier you start the better. People who were effective in their careers usually had clear, firm goals and plans. A successful retirement is no different.

For many, "retirement" is more of a transition rather than a destination. After a brief break and rest-up period, many Baby Boomers are ready to tackle the next phase in their lives. For some, the next phase is public service and volun-teerism. For others, it means pursuing the career they always wanted but had to shelve because it didn't pay enough to raise a family. Your focus in retirement often reflects your true passion. This is a good time to review your "bucket list" and move some items into the active column.

An MSNBC study reported on a man who was a Director in the Tax Department of a Big Four accounting firm. He was able to retire at age 60 with full benefits, but felt that he still had much to accomplish in life. He wrote a list of the things he wanted out of his retirement: to give back to the community, personal fulfillment, keep active. His choice of what to do in retirement was to become a medic in the town he had raised his family. At age 62, he is now a part of the local dispatch team. He said he could not have thought of a better way to spend his retirement.

THE FIRST DAY OF THE REST OF YOUR LIFE

Today, age 65 is no longer old. When Roosevelt instituted this artificial retirement age, life expectancy was 62. Now, average life expectancy is creeping towards 80, and many people who are retiring at 65 are blessed with good health, energy and undiminished imagination.

People who are 65 still feel like they have a lot to offer, and don't intend to spend the rest of their lives watching television or refining their golf game. One of our clients is in her mid-70s, has ample pension income and more than enough assets to retire, but is still working. She feels that working keeps her young, and has the attitude, "Use it or lose it."

Retirement as we currently know it was crafted in the Industrial Age, when mass production made it easy to replace older, burnt-out workers with younger, more energetic ones. A mandatory retirement age enforced this changing of the guard. Today, in the Information Age, this model makes less sense. Now it is knowledge and experience that are more important than strength and reflexes. A retiring 65-year-old is very valuable. Companies find that they are losing their most essential workers to retirement. Their retirement leaves gaping holes in the company's resources that a 20-something new employee cannot easily fill.

Some retirees now mentor younger employees in order to pass on their experience, knowledge and skills to upcoming workers.

RETIREMENT & MARITAL HARMONY

Ironically, some couples who looked forward to spending more time together in retirement unexpectedly find that it is a time of increased marital stress. Japanese call it the Sticky-Leaf syndrome – wives find their husbands tagging along everywhere, demanding attention. They complain, "Whenever I turn around, there he is!"

To avoid falling into this syndrome, plan ahead. Imagine that you are already retired and create a Model Week for yourself. List all the activities that you would typically engage in. After you enter your golf time, maintaining your house and garden, and any other leisure activities, take a look at the vast amount of time you have left. An anonymous author once wrote, "Leisure is a beautiful garment, but it will not do for constant wear."

When one or both spouses find interests outside of the home, whether it is part time work, consulting, or volunteerism, marital harmony often returns to normal.

CLOSE THE LOOP BY GIVING BACK

A sedentary life sometimes leads to feelings of purposelessness, boredom, and reduced self-esteem. It can even be a death sentence to someone who has much to contribute but no outlet for his or her talents. Many people are happiest when they are giving themselves to something larger than themselves. In many cases, this means giving back.

One of the most rewarding aspects of retirement is the opportunity to close the loop and help some of the groups or people who helped you. It may give you some ideas if you ask yourself these questions:

- How can you use your insights and experience to benefit others?
- What causes, organizations or individuals have made a difference in your life?

Answering these questions will lead you to the intersection of where your skills and experience can help the organizations you feel the most passionate about.

CREATE TIME FOR GROWTH

In order to enjoy retirement, you want to delegate the activities that you don't like to do yourself, and others can do better and faster than you. Conversely, you want to concentrate on what you can't delegate – having fun and enjoying life, spending time with your family, maintaining your health, entering a new phase of growth.

Check out where you want to live. If you are thinking of moving to another location for retirement, try to spend as much time as possible there in all types of seasons and weather conditions before you actually move. If possible, rent in the area before you buy a home.

A television documentary on retirement followed a couple who spent the last 35 years of their lives in the North East. They dreamed of retiring in the warmer weather of Florida one day. So in retirement, they bought their dream home in Key West – it was everything they had hoped. Two years later, the couple was back in their home town of Hartford, Connecticut. The wife said, "I thought, more than anything, I wanted to retire in Key West. When I was there, I found myself flying back to Hartford every other weekend because I missed my grandkids. After two years of the back and forth, we decided it was time to go back 'home' where our kids were."

Many people are determined that their brains are not going to go into retirement when they do. An increasing number of people are planning to retire in college towns. They like the intellectual stimulation, the cultural offerings and the often excellent medical facilities. They'll be attending classes and in some cases, earning degrees in areas of study they've been passionate about for years but couldn't devote time to until retirement.

We may even have to toss out the term "retirement" and replace it with a concept that encompasses achievement of our lifetime goals in growth, health, meaningfulness, and happiness. Mark Twain had it right when he said, "Twenty years from now you will be more disappointed by the things you didn't do than by the ones you did do. So throw off the bowlines. Sail away from the harbor. Catch the trade winds in your sails. Explore. Dream. Discover."

INDEX

Alan Kondo, a specialist in retirement and estate planning, is a Certified Financial Planner™ (CFP), Chartered Life Underwriter (CLU), and Certified Collaborative Advisor (CCA). Kondo Wealth Advisors, LLC (KWA), provides investment management and risk management as well as advisory services for retirement planning, estate planning and charitable planning.

He is a regular columnist in the *Rafu Shimpo* on retirement and estate planning topics. He is the author of the book *Path to Antei, A Japanese American Guide to Financial Success* and a contributing author on *Giving: Philanthropy for Everyone.*

He received his Bachelor's degree at the University of Toronto, and his Master's degree from Loyola Marymount University. Originally from Toronto, Canada, he is married to Ruth Wakabayashi, a retired teacher with the Los Angeles Unified School District. They have three daughters, Kimiko, Akemi and Masayo. He continues to give his time and talent generously to community organizations such as Keiro Senior Healthcare, Little Tokyo Service Center, Japanese American Community and Cultural Center, Japanese American National Museum, East San Gabriel Valley Japanese Community Center, and Japanese American Cultural and Community Center Northern California.

Alan was a recipient of the Steven Tatsukawa Memorial Fund Award, given to individuals committed to the progress of the Asian Pacific American community. He was a key creative force in Visual Communications, an Asian Pacific media and resource center.

Before going independent as a Registered Investment Advisor, KWA was Transamerica's top Advisory Firm and received Transamerica's Leading Producer Award as well as the Outstanding Advisory Services Achievement Award. KWA became an independent Registered Investment Advisor in 2011 motivated by Alan's goal to "have our clients be our only boss" and better achieve their goals with trusted advice, considerate care and the best financial strategies available.

Akemi Kondo Dalvi is a Financial Advisor in the field of retirement planning and investment management. She has worked with Kondo Wealth Advisors, LLC (KWA), a professional wealth management practice since 2008. Akemi is also employed as a Registered Representative of Purshe Kaplan Sterling Investments, Inc. (PKS), a registered broker-dealer and Member FINRA/SIPC. Akemi is an Investment Advisor Representative in the state of California.

Prior to working as a Financial Advisor, Akemi worked at PricewaterhouseCoopers, LLP (PwC), a global professional services firm. She joined Transamerica in 2008. In 2010, Akemi received her Series 7 license as a General Securities Representative and her Series 66 license as an Investment Advisor Representative. Akemi holds the professional designation of Certified Public Accountant (CPA) awarded in 2008 by the California Board of Accountancy. Akemi is also licensed to sell life insurance and long term care in the state of California. Akemi is a member of the Financial Planning Association and the American Institute of Certified Public Accountants.

Akemi was born in Los Angeles, California. She received her Bachelor of Science degree from the University of Southern California in the field of Accounting. She is married to Ashay and they have a son, Aiden.

CONTACT INFORMATION:

Kondo Wealth Advisors, LLC
300 N. Lake Ave. #920
Pasadena, CA 91101
626-449-7783
www.kondowealthadvisors.com
Email: info@kondowealthadvisors.com

QUICK ORDER FORM

Fax Orders: 626-449-7785. Send this form.
Telephone Orders: 626-449-7783
Email Orders: info@kondowealthadvisors.com
Postal Orders: Kondo Wealth Advisors
                               300 N. Lake Ave. #920
                               Pasadena, CA 91101

Please send the following books.

Quantity _____ *Retiring Upstream: Finding Happiness and*
                          Security in the Transition of a Lifetime **($19.95)**

Name: _____

Address: _____

City: _____ State: _____ Zip:_____

Telephone: _____

Email:_____

Sales Tax: Please add 9% to your order.

Shipping by air:
    U.S.: $6.00 first book; $2.00 each additional.
    International: $12.00 first book; $5.00 each additional.

Payment: ☐ Check   ☐ Visa   ☐ Mastercard

Card number: _____

Exp. date:_____ 3-digit security code (on back of card) _____

Name on card: _____